Blue and Gold Macaws

Blue and Gold Macaws as pets.

Blue and Gold Macaw book for Keeping, Care, Housing, Diet, Health. Pros and Cons.
by

Roger Rodendale

Table of Contents

Introduction

Macaws are among the most popular pet birds in the world. These birds are known for being extremely colorful and visually appealing. There are large, small and hybrid varieties of these birds. Currently 11 large varieties, 6 small varieties and over 35 hybrid varieties of these birds exist, giving bird lovers a large selection to choose from.

Of all the types of macaws, Blue and Gold Macaws have risen to popularity because these birds are extremely intelligent and highly trainable in addition to being brightly colored. These birds are classified under the large macaw species.

Also known as the Bolivian Blue and Gold Macaws, these birds are a force to be reckoned with. Along with being large birds, they also have humongous personalities. They make great companions to their owners because of their friendly and sensitive personality. They are known for being very loving and also love to cuddle and play.

While the personality of these birds can make it very tempting to bring one home, one needs to understand the correct way of caring for them. When stressed and uncared for, these birds tend to develop several health issues as well as behavioral issues. Behavioral issues include biting or screaming. With a bird as big as the Blue and Gold macaw, behavioral issues can become hazardous to you and your family members.

Before you bring home a Blue and Gold Macaw, ensure that you learn about the requirements of these birds so that you are able to provide them with adequate care. These exotic birds have specific dietary requirements that you need to cater to in order to keep them healthy. They also need good housing and maintenance.

In addition to this, these birds are highly intelligent, which means that you need to learn about the right ways to keep them engaged and mentally active. There are several options including toys and training that you can read about in this book.

This book takes you through the natural history and the care requirements of these birds. That way, you know what to expect when you bring a Blue and Gold macaw home. You have a complete guide to assist you from the time you bring the bird home. This book covers important subjects such as creating the perfect housing area for your pet, the right diet, necessary health precautions, tips to handle your bird, training and a lot more.

The goal is to make sure that you get information that has been collected from macaw owners. Hence, all the tips that you find in this book are authentic and are easy to apply. As you spend time with your beloved pet, you too will learn more about his or her behavior and figure out your own unique way of bonding and interacting with the bird.

For novices in the world of macaws, this book is a great way to get a head start so that you and your bird can enjoy a wonderful journey together.

Chapter 1: Meet the Blue and Gold Macaw

Originally from Bolivia, the Blue and Gold Macaw is counted as the most popular species of macaw that is kept as a pet because of its big personality and beautiful plumage.

These birds make great companions and are extremely interactive. Their high intelligence makes them one of the most trainable of all the macaw species. To make sure that you provide proper care for these birds, it is very important to understand the natural history and behavior of these birds. That way, you will be able to create an environment that is not only conducive for these birds but also helps them thrive into healthier individuals.

1. Physical traits of the Blue and Gold Macaw

Blue and Gold Macaws are large birds that are known for their brightly colored feathers. These birds can be distinguished from other macaw species by the following physical traits:

- **Plumage:** They have the most vividly colored plumes. The back, back of the head and wings have mostly turquoise-blue colored feathers. The top of the head has bright emerald green feathers. The tips of the wings also have green feathering. The front of the body has bright yellow colored feathers. Sometimes the feathers below the chest can acquire an orange hue because of the dirt of the bird or other environmental factors. The throat and the chin vary from black to dark blue in color.

- **Face:** The face of these birds is bare with a white mask. You will see lines of single black feathers around the eyes that merge into a black collar just below the neck. The face tends to turn a pinkish shade when the bird is excited. As the birds age, you will see wrinkles on their face.

- **Eyes:** In the case of adults, the eyes are pale yellow in color and in the case of juveniles, they are dark.

- **Beak:** These birds have massive beaks that are strong and hooked. The beak is usually dark grey or black in color. The beak is extremely powerful, allowing them to crack open nuts and also use it as a third limb when climbing.

- **Tongue:** The tongue of the Blue and Gold Macaw is all black.
- **Toes:** These birds have zygodactylous feet. This means that they have two toes that point forward and two toes that point backwards. This is an adaptation that gives these birds better grip when they are perching on tree branches.

- **Tail:** They have a long tail that is pointed at the tips. The top of the tail is blue in color while the under parts are golden in color.

- **Size and Weight:** As mentioned before, these birds are massive in their size. Adults may grow up to 32-35 inches in length from the head to the tip of the tail. The wingspan ranges from 41-45 inches. An adult bird usually weighs about 1 to 1.8 kilos.

These birds are not sexually dimorphic. This means that the male and the female look similar to each other. There are a few physical differences that are observed. For instance, the frame of the female is more slender. The heads of the males tend to be flatter and the beaks of the females are narrower.

However, the only way to surely determine the gender of the bird is through DNA sexing or through surgical sexing.

Even the juvenile birds look identical to the adults. However, they have darker eyes that are usually grey or brown in color.

Similar species: Blue and Gold Macaws are strikingly similar to Blue Throated Macaws. However, the difference lies in the blue throat patch that is only seen in the latter. The Blue Throated Macaw is also entirely blue in color and has facial skin that is slightly reddish in color. The face and the throat patch are the two factors that help you distinguish between these birds easily.

2. Natural range and Habitat

The natural range of these birds is expansive. Although these birds are believed to be native to Bolivia, you can see populations extending from Southern Central America to Eastern Panama and Colombia, excluding West Narino and Cauca Valley. They also inhabit areas between Southern and Eastern Venezuela, Brazil, French Guinea, Western and Eastern Ecuador, Eastern parts of Peru and the North Eastern parts of Bolivia.

These birds were also found in North Argentina, Paraguay, Western areas of Ecuador and the Trinidad Islands. These birds were last recorded in these areas in the 1960s.

Several populations have been introduced to Puerto Rico, Mexico and South Florida. These populations have established themselves quite strongly in these areas.

Large populations of these birds have diminished over the years because of illegal capture for pet trade, loss of habitat and also overhunting by the locals.

These birds mostly inhabit the rain forests where they make their nests in the lowlands up to 500 meters above sea level. Their other habitats include marshlands, open savannahs, riversides and swamps.

These birds are usually seen in pairs or in small groups on the higher branches of large trees. In late afternoons and mornings, several groups club together to form noisy flocks that move from one feeding ground to another.

3. Taxonomy

Blue and Gold Macaws are considered to be monotypic birds. This means that only one species of these birds exist. However, this has been questioned time and again by the scientific community. As a result, the classification of the Bolivian Blue and Gold Macaw as Ara*ararauna*is is still under research. There have been some discussions and changes that have been named over the years.

The common name of this species, Blue and Gold Macaw, is sometimes even used to identify the Blue Throated Macaw. However, these birds are not differentiated as sub species currently. They have commonly been associated with one another. This is likely to be revised in the near future, as research is still ongoing.

As of now, the Bolivian Blue and Gold Macaw is distinguished by its larger size. These birds are sometimes even larger than the Hyacinth

Macaw and the Green Wing Macaw although these species are among the largest macaws. The blue color of these birds is also described as "True Blue" in comparison to turquoise or green blue coloration seen in the Blue Throated Macaw.

Many believe that the Blue and Gold Macaw is a result of selective breeding that involved a Blue Throated Macaw in the mix. This theory has been questioned, as the Blue and Gold Macaw is much larger. According to hybridization theories, creating a specimen that is larger than the parents is usually unsuccessful.

According to ornithologist Joseph Forshaw from Australia, there is a good chance that the Blue Throated Macaw is a sub species of the Blue and Gold Macaw. This theory was based on the fact that many Blue Throated Macaws have been found in the southern regions of the range covered by Blue and Gold Macaws. It is also possible as the two species are strikingly similar to one another.

The Blue Throated Macaw differs because of its smaller size, lesser bare area on the face, the broad markings on the cheeks and the characteristic blue patch on the throat.

This theory is very recent and is often debated. For a long time the Blue Throated Macaw was considered an abnormal variety of the Blue and Gold Macaw. However, there are no records of the two species ever breeding with one another even in areas where their ranges seem to overlap with one another. They are also physically quite different from one another. As a result, the current conclusion is that these are two different, mutually exclusive species.

4. Personality and behavior

In the wild, Blue and Gold Macaws make large flocks that are very close knit. They are known to form extremely strong bonds with their mates. You will often see these birds bathing and playing with their mates and also gathering ripe fruits together.

Like most macaw species, Blue and Gold Macaws also love being around their flock mates. They will only branch away from their flock during the breeding season. They form separate nests where they can raise their young. The nests are usually made in the hollows of trees or in palm trees that the female cleans out before laying any eggs. They find nesting sites that are well guarded and safe.

When the babies arrive, the mother and the father feed the babies until they fledge. Until the babies begin to feather out, the mother stays in the nest with them. She then leaves them to search for food as the food demands also increase as the birds fledge. Typically, the babies stay with the parents for a little over three months and then move out on their own.

In captivity, Blue and Gold Macaws are abundant as they are high in demand. The personality of these birds is very unique and interesting, making them a preferred choice for those looking for a companion bird.

They are also very common in animal parks and bird shows because of their size and the striking plumage. They are known to draw large crowds, as they can perform several tricks and truly entertain.

Every bird has a unique personality, just like human beings. The behavior of Blue and Gold Macaws vary quite a bit depending upon his mental state, the health conditions and also his surroundings. They are extremely intelligent birds. They are known for being curious, playful, friendly and mildly temperamental. (Please note, although there are female varieties, we will refer to them as "he" for ease).

The good news is that since these birds are highly intelligent, they are quite easy to train. If you have brought home a younger bird, especially, you will be able to socialize and train them a lot better. Taking good care of the physical and mental health of macaws is of utmost importance, as they may develop behavioral issues when care is inadequate. There are several issues such as aggression, noisiness and also extreme territorial behavior.

If you are someone who has very little time and travels frequently, then the macaw is not the right bird for you. These birds need time in order to thrive well. If you do not want any loud noises then the bird is not right for you either. These birds are quite vocal and may also resort to loud calls and screams when they are excited or at dusk. You also need to make sure that you have space in your home to house these birds without causing any inconvenience to other family members or your neighbors.

Blue and Gold Macaws are the best talkers among all the species of macaws. They are able to learn several words and phrases. They are also expressive, using different verbal and non-verbal methods of communication.

Often, macaws get the reputation of being reserved and shy birds. They are less interactive at a younger age. As they grow, they tend to become more curious. They love to explore and also understand how their behavior can affect your behavior. In fact, they learn things like how to get you into a room or how to get your attention, so make sure that you train and socialize your bird to ensure that he does not manipulate you.

If you treat the Blue and Gold Macaw as a member of your family, they will give you endless love and affection. It is a two way street. The more you are committed to your bird emotionally, the more you get in return. This is a relationship that you will have to maintain for at least 30 years. It is necessary to also have someone to take care of the bird in case the owner is old. That way if the owner passes before the bird, the latter is not left abandoned.

These birds are extremely entertaining. They love to go out with their owners, spend time with them, solve puzzles, climb around the cage or even hang from their perches.

Remember to socialize your macaw as early as you can. Since these birds are large, the danger is higher. These birds tend to get excited and may even nip playfully. However, because their beaks are large and powerful, there are chances of serious injuries. The more time you spend training your bird, the safer it is to have them as pets.

5. Natural diet

The natural diet of macaws consists of a variety of nuts, fruits, seeds and other plant material. They tend to have a diet that is richer in fat. This is because these birds require a lot of energy that they use while going in search of food from one place to another. They also tend to fly for miles to find mates and even to rear their chicks.

In case of any scarcity in food, macaws tend to eat raw fruits or may even eat plants that are toxic to them. This may lead to upset stomachs and infections. However, the birds combat this by licking clay off the riverbeds. This clay, it is believed, enriches the system of the birds with certain minerals they are lacking because fruits and seeds are sparse. This helps them flush out toxins and stay healthy as well.

The theories behind clay licking
The different sites in which these birds lick clay are of utmost importance to biologists and also to tourists. The birds gather in flocks of hundreds, often including other parrot species. It is a great ground to conduct studies and also attracts people from different parts of the world to witness this unique spectacle.

However, the question that still remains is, why do macaws lick clay? Earlier studies showed that the clay helps flush out tannins and other toxins that are usually obtained from plants. The clay helps neutralize the tannins. It binds to the toxins before it can be absorbed by the digestive tract. That way, the toxins are excreted along with the clay.

There are other reports that suggest that the clay allows the birds to cope with a diet that is poor in sodium. This is because the peculiar behavior is often restricted to birds that are found in the Western Amazon regions. This is often connected to the lack of salts in the Amazon basin. This is also an area that has heavy rainfall, leading to the salt being leaked out of the soil.

These areas very important in terms of tourism. In fact, one such area at the Many National Park and Biosphere Reserve in Peru has been recognized as a World Heritage Site by the UNESCO. There are over 800 species of birds and 200 species of mammals in this park alone. Out of them six different species of macaws gather around these clay licks, making for a magnificent sight.

6. Conservation status

The Gold and Blue Macaw is listed in the Appendix II of CITES. This means that, in the wild, these birds are of Least Concern. However, there isn't enough evidence to suggest how many birds actually occur in the wild. These birds have often been described as uncommon.

That said, Blue and Gold Macaws still face several threats in the wild such as habitat loss, illegal capture for pet trade and also hunting. Several attempts have been made to reintroduce these birds to the wild to increase their population. However, these efforts have adverse effects for the birds that are native to the region where reintroduction is attempted.

Several studies conducted on Blue and Gold Macaw populations have revealed that the breeding output of these birds is quite low. Bonded pairs do not necessarily breed every year. Studies show that breeding groups with almost 100 adults can only produce up to 15 young every year. Out of these the survival rate is not 100% either.

Another potential threat to the populations of these birds is the dependence swamps with Aguaje Palm. The fruit of this tree is also used abundantly by locals who reside around it. In the 1980s, according to research, the people of Iquitos in Peru required close to 15 tons of this fruit every day in particular seasons.

As a result, whole trees are cut down to harvest these fruits. Dead palms, that form the best nesting sites for these birds, are able to only last for about 7 years. Then, these trees simply fall to the ground. As a result, nest availability and competition for food sources are also major threats to the populations of these birds in the wild.

The biggest threat to date for these birds remains the fact that they make great pets. They have a high taming potential and have the most beautiful plumage. These birds are also able to mimic human voices, making them more desirable.

There are several zoos and private institutions that try to safeguard this species from extinction with the help of captive breeding. These breeding programs are very well scheduled and also have special studbook keepers to monitor them. Usually, breeding is used as a means to meet the commercial demand for these birds. The result of this is that there are large populations thriving in captivity. As a result, there is no need for any more birds to be captured in the wild for pet trade.

However, captive breeding comes with several drawbacks. There are breeders who opt for the most unethical means to get breed these birds just to meet the demands. This leads to birds that are poor in health, with the ability to contaminate any aviary that they are introduced to.

Peru is known for its continuous efforts to save the populations of these birds. The main focus remains on nest creation. Several Aguaje Palms were selected carefully and the tops were cut. The hollow of the trees were occupied in about 5-12 months by the Blue and Gold Macaws. In each of these hollows 7 chicks were produced each year before the tree finally fell to the ground.

These palm cuttings are planned carefully and also keep the local human population in mind. They also ensure that no other wildlife species that inhabit the swamp areas are affected. This is a conservation technique that is believed to be long term. It is effective in naturally restoring the wild populations and making these birds more common.

There are also several laws that have been imposed on the import and export of these birds to safeguard their populations.

7. Long live the Blue and Gold Macaw

If you are planning to bring home a Blue and Gold Macaw, this is one of the most important things for you to know. These birds have a really long lifespan, longer than any other species of macaws.

Some birds have also lived for more than 60 years. On average, the life span of Blue and Gold Macaws is about 35 years in captivity.

In the year 1899, a Blue and Gold Macaw was born. This female macaw named Charlie celebrated her 112th birthday in the year 2011. It is believed that Charlie was once the pet of Winston Churchill. The bird became popular for her anti-nazi slogans and cursing. Her final home was the Heathfield Nursery in Great Britain.

The Guinness Book, however, records Cookie, a Cockatoo belonging to Major Mitchell, as the longest living parrot. She is believed to have lived for 83 years.

The maximum age of these birds is the result of good breeding conditions and good care. They do not live as long in the wild because their nests as well as their little ones are under threat by predators like the Harpy Eagle, Orange Crested Falcon, Hawk Eagle and also snakes. Of course, wild populations are also threatened by several human activities.

Chapter 2: 10 Things to Know Before Bringing One Home

Bringing a bird like the Blue and Gold Macaw home requires you to be well prepared. The transition from the source that you buy your bird from to your home is very stressful. If you are unprepared, it only adds to it and can make the bird ill or may lead to unpleasant behavior that can be dangerous.

In addition to that, knowing what your bird needs to be healthy will tell you if you are really ready for one or not. If you are not able to manage these ten basic requirements of the Blue and Gold Macaw, you may want to wait for a while before you make the commitment. Remember, you will have to sustain them all for well over 30 years.

1. They need great housing
A bird like the Blue and Gold Macaw is not exactly easy to house. When you are preparing to bring a bird home, you need to makes sure that the housing area is ready for the bird to move into as soon as it reaches your home.

Housing a Blue and Gold Macaw is a challenge owing to the sheer size of the bird. It isn't enough to just build a cage for the bird and leave him there. There are several factors that you need to consider in order to keep the bird comfortable in your home:

The depth of the tail and the wingspan
Your Blue and Gold Macaw should be able to stretch in the cage easily. The wingspan of the bird is about 3-4 feet in length on average. The minimum size of the cage should be such that your bird is able to spread his wings without touching the sides of the cage. The tail is also long, so you have to make sure that it does not get entangled in the bars of the cage.

The minimum size requirement for a Blue and Gold Macaw cage is a depth of 30 inches, height of 60-72 inches and a width of 48 inches. If you are able to get a cage that actually allows your bird to fly, it is called a true flight cage. This would ideally be about twice the size of the dimensions mentioned above.

In case of large macaws, the most important factor is the depth. Most breeders recommend that the deeper the cage, the better it is for the bird, although it makes it hard to handle the bird and reach out. The key to keeping your bird in a deep cage is to train them well to step up.

Strong beaks need strong cages
A fully-grown Blue and Gold Macaw can easily chew his way through the cage if the bars are not sturdy enough. There are several kinds of cages made from different material that you will find at pet stores. The best option for a bird like the Blue and Gold Macaw is a stainless steel one.

Most Blue and Gold Macaw breeders will tell you that material is certainly important, but what you need to focus on more is the construction of the cage. If you are certain that the cage is welded properly, then you can be sure of your bird's safety. Another type of construction is square tubing, which is sturdier. However, it is harder to clean.

The ideal diameter of the bar is about ¼ inches and the distance between them should be between ½ to 2 inches. In case of a 2-inch spacing between the bar, you will be able to see the bird better. It also helps the bird climb the cage easily. However, if the spacing is too much, it may lead to the tail getting entangled and will also reduce the grip that your bird gets to climb and stay active enough during their time inside the cage.

On the other hand, if you are able to provide your bird with a cage that is large enough, he is less likely to want to chew. He will stay entertained and will be a lot easier for you to train to behave well, too.

Keeping them busy
The cage ought to be the bird's haven. If he does not enjoy going back into the cage, chances are that he will fuss around to go back in after being trained to step up or step out.

For this, you need to give the bird a lot of toys that he can chew on, climb and just play with. There are several things like soft wood that you can give your bird to also keep the beak in good condition.

At the same time, make sure that the cage does not get overcrowded. If your bird is constantly hitting his head against the toys, it is an indication that there are too many. If a bird as large as the Blue and Gold Macaw is able to hide behind these toys, it is also a sign that you need to go easy on the toys. Lastly, the bird needing to actually walk through a maze of toys to get to his food is also an indication that you have gone overboard with the number of toys in the cage.

Be prepared for a big mess
A bird as big as a Blue and Gold Macaw is bound to make a big mess. So, make sure that the cage floor is made of material that is easy to clean up. It doesn't matter if it is an indoor or outdoor cage, being easy to clean is the key. This also ensures that your birds are in the peak of their health at all times.

Surfaces like plastic, tile and concrete are great and are really easy to clean. The best option is chair mats made of plastic that are normally used on office chairs. They cannot be torn and eaten by the bird. In addition, there is no risk of the bird hurting himself on a hard surface.

If you have an aviary, it is best that you include a drain in it. The more birds you have, the more the mess. The drain will also make it easier when you wash the aviary once every 15-20 days.

Placing the perches in the cage
The toes of your Blue and Gold Macaws stay in shape and stay protected when you have proper perches in the cage. You can get a good variety of these perches in pet stores. You need to make sure that your bird can get all of his toes around the perch for him to benefit from it. The ideal size of a perch is up to 2 inches in diameter. You can also get flat perches that will serve as resting perches.

You may choose to hang these perches vertically as well. That makes for a fun activity for your macaw. Watch as they hang on to the perch and climb. The best material for these perches is soft wood that is also safe for the birds to chew on.

Food and water containers

The Blue and Gold Macaw is a large bird, so it is necessary for you to provide him with containers that are large and sturdy enough to eat from. Some owners actually use dog dishes made from stainless steel. All you need is material that is easy to clean and sturdy. The ideal size for the food and water containers of Blue and Gold Macaws is 3 inches in depth and about 8 inches in diameter.

You can even make feeding time fun by adding foraging boxes near the food and water containers. They can even be cardboard boxes that you place food in and make the birds work for it. This box can be changed everyday in case your bird begins to chew on it! This should be for special foods only, so add a treat or your bird's favorite food. The harder you make it for them to access the food, the longer they will stay entertained!

Cage maintenance

It is not enough that you have a beautiful birdcage in your home. You need to make sure that you take good care of this cage and keep it clean to ensure good health of the bird. Of course, no one would want to have a smelly birdcage into their room. There are different frequencies of cleaning for each part of the cage. This is your guide to proper birdcage maintenance:

- **Everyday cleaning:** You will have to spend a few minutes each day examining the cage and making sure that it is in good condition. On a daily basis, you will have to replace the substrate that you have placed on the floor of the cage. You will also have to make sure that the food and water bowls are cleaned and the contents are changed every single day.

  If you notice any toy with a lot of poop on it, it will have to be cleaned immediately. In the case of food that has been spilled, fruits and vegetables should not be allowed to stay for more than one hour in the cage. Eating a small piece of rotting fruit or vegetable can cause GI tract infections almost immediately.

- **Fortnightly cleaning:** Every 15 days, a complete wipe down of the cage is necessary. Using any antibacterial cleaner that you can get in any pet store, wipe the floor and the bars of the cage. Dirty toys can also be wiped with the same liquid. This cleaning practice must be followed regularly to reduce the breeding grounds for microbes and thus reduce the chances of infection. If the cage is damp, remove the bird from the cage and allow the cage to dry naturally in the sun for a few minutes before replacing the bird.

- **Monthly cleaning:** Whether you have an aviary or just a single cage, this monthly through cleaning is a must. First, you need to place the bird in a temporary cage or enclosure. Then, all the accessories including the chains that are used to hold these toys up should be removed and soaked in an antibacterial solution or even mild soap water.

  The cage should be cleaned thoroughly. First, any dried feces or debris should be scraped out. Following this, the cage should be washed completely using soapy water. For those who prefer natural cleaning agents, diluted vinegar is a great option.

  Make sure that the toys and the cage are rinsed thoroughly to remove any traces of soap. After that, you can allow them to dry in the sun before you replace them in the cage. You will let the bird into the cage only after everything is fully dry.

This cleaning schedule is quite easy to follow and is usually preferred by most bird owners. You will have a clean and hygienic cage that is free from disease-causing microbes. In addition to that, keeping an indoor cage clean is a must to keep your family healthy as well.

2. A varied diet is a must

Even in the wild, Blue and Gold Macaws eat a variety of foods. Therefore, if you want to keep them healthy, make sure that you go beyond a regular seed diet.

What to include

- The seeds that you can use include pumpkin seeds, fennel seeds, safflower seeds and sunflower seeds.

- Nuts that are best suited for Blue and Gold Macaws are cashews, brazil nuts, macadamia nuts, pine nuts, walnuts, almonds and filberts.

- There are several greens, fruits and vegetables that can be included in the diet such as papaya, corn, soy beans, mangoes, pears, peaches, apple, carrot, pineapple, apricots, broccoli, thyme, bell peppers, celery, spinach, raspberries and basil.

- Any veggies that contain many oxalates should be given to the Blue and Gold Macaw in moderation. This includes bokchoy, spinach and even chard. This is because the absorption of calcium is compromised with these foods.

- Fruits that contain too much sugar must be avoided entirely.

- Any food that is 100% cooked, including beans, pasta or grains. These foods tend to have more calories and are also high in phosphorous. This puts your bird at the risk of becoming obese, so offer sparingly.

- Seeds should be provided occasionally or as treats, most preferably. This is because they have very little nutritional value and are high in fats.

Remember that avocados can be poisonous for your bird and must never be included in the diet. If you want to provide your bird with raisins, it should be given in small quantities only in order for your bird to get maximum benefits.

In general, all macaws need to have a higher level of fat in their diet. This can be ensured to your bird by giving them nuts as an integral part of their diet. As for the fruits and vegetables, you can try a large variety for your bird. You will see that they will pick their likes and dislikes.

What to avoid
- Caffeine

- Chocolate

- Alcohol

- Pits of fruits like apricots, plums, peaches and nectarines. This leads to vomiting or even coma, as these pits contain enzyme inhibitors.

- Green potatoes, tomato leaves and eggplant contain poisonous alkaloids. They may lead to diarrhea, vomiting and even difficulty in breathing.

- Raw beans should never be given to macaws as it hampers their protein metabolism. In addition to that, it also contains other toxins that can harm the bird. Giving your bird cooked beans occasionally is a better option.

- Nutmeg is a complete no as it contains myristicin, which makes your bird nauseous and dizzy. It can also cause vomiting in birds immediately after consumption.

- Rhubarb leaves are extremely toxic to birds. They contain an intestinal irritant called oxalic acid. If your bird consumes large doses of this compound, it could be lethal.

- Do not allow your bird to ingest tobacco fumes or eat the leaves. This leads to seizures, diarrhea and more severe symptoms. Basically, if you are a smoker, you will want to keep your bird as far away from the smoking area of your home as possible.

Occasional treats

- Baby food: Human baby food along with fresh fruits and vegetables make a great base mix for your bird.

- Dried produce: If you are unable to source fresh produce, you can give your bird dried vegetables and fruits. In fact, birds enjoy the fact that these foods are crunchy. You also have the option of soaking these foods in warm water. This, it is believed, reminds the birds of the regurgitated foods given to them by parents, which is also moist and warm. These foods help birds progress from seeds to a healthier diet option.

You need to make sure that any food that you are giving your bird has no artificial coloring. This is usually done to make foods visually more attractive and can be harmful in terms of nutrition. The other thing to avoid is sulfur dioxide. Check the labels thoroughly to ensure that your foods do not have any traces of this chemical. It may make your bird hyper active, can increase aggressive behavior and can even lead to feather plucking or shedding. Allergic reactions to these additives can have mild to severe symptoms that you need to watch out for.

The most convenient food option for Blue and Gold Macaws is sprouted seeds. This is when you do not have time to prepare the base mix with veggies, seeds, etc. An equal portion of these sprouted seeds can be very nutritious. In addition to that, birds simply love sprouted seeds and these are a great way to introduce greens to your bird.
Blue and Gold Macaws are large birds who need good nutrition and good portions of the right nutrients in order for them to thrive. If you are uncertain about what you must give your bird, you may even consult your

vet or an experienced Blue and Gold Macaw owner. However, never assume that what is good for you must be good for the bird. They have different requirements in terms of diet and you need to be careful about maintaining a balance of all the nutrients that they need.

3. You need to take ample safety measures

There are many common hazards around the house that you need to take care of before you bring a Blue and Gold Macaw home. While bird proofing your house is necessary, you also need to make sure that your family knows how to handle and care for the bird, for their safety and the safety of the bird. Remember that you are dealing with a very large sized bird.

Safety begins by preparing your family for a bird. Then, make sure your house is fully bird proofed before you bring one home.

Preparing the family

It is natural for members of your family, especially the little ones, to want to play with the Blue and Gold Macaw. After all, it is such a pretty bird and everyone will want to put their fingers through the cage and try to touch the bird. This will stress him out a lot, so it is a good idea to lay down a few guidelines to the family when you bring a new Blue and Gold Macaw home:

- Leave the bird alone. Everyone should be asked to refrain from approaching the cage, tapping on it or crowding around it.

- Do not talk to the bird. This is the most important instruction. Saying hello in different voices is more stressful that you can imagine for your Blue and Gold Macaw.

- Do not introduce new people to the house and allow them to play or approach the bird. You see, a Blue and Gold Macaw, as beautiful as it is, is not an object that you want to show off. It is a bird that can get really scared and develop health issues with stress.

- No pictures and selfies! The flash from your camera or even the sound made by the camera can be a trigger for aggressive behavior. You will always have several opportunities to take pictures of the Blue and Gold Macaw. Just be sure that you do not do that on the first day of the bird's arrival into your home.

- No loud music. On the first day, especially, the Blue and Gold Macaw needs a lot of calm and quiet. Keep him in a room that has less traffic noises.

- Do not slam doors shut. Sudden noises are not appreciated by Blue and Gold Macaws. They are really frightened by these sudden and loud noises.

- No large or colorful toys near the cage. This can also aggravate the stress for your bird. Children do things like taking their teddy bears close to the cage and saying, "Boo!" This should never be done. Not on the first day or any other day.

- Prepare your family for the fact that your Blue and Gold Macaw can be a screamer. He may scream all night long. This is his way of displaying fear. He may also be calling out to the other birds in the aviary or to his previous owner. It will subside if you do not disturb the bird and keep him calm.

- Do not feed the bird from your hands on the first day. In fact, you need to tell them not to approach the cage with treats for a few days. This may induce biting or nipping as the birds go straight for the fingers. And if someone shouts or screams when he does this, the bird feels encouraged!

- No one should handle the bird. Even the most experienced bird owners should not handle your Blue and Gold Macaw on the first day.

Keeping the bird safe

Every macaw pet owner has an obligation to exercise caution whenever they allow birds some freedom in the house. Many seemingly innocent common household furnishings can be dangerous for macaws.

If no one is at home to monitor the bird, it is best to keep it caged. This is because the freedom can be a recipe for harm. Think of a macaw gnawing on electric cables or on your library of favorite books; that is danger and losses.

Make sure you take the following precautions:

- Windows and mirrors do not appear to be a barrier to flying birds. They may unwittingly proceed headfirst into them, possibly causing severe injury or loss of consciousness. If the birds are able to fly free, try to keep these surfaces covered.

- Do not keep doors and windows open. The danger is obvious. The loss of a pet bird is not uncommon due to this and can easily be avoided if proper precautions are taken well in advance.

- Birds are always at risk of drowning. The precaution is to ensure that all water containers remain adequately covered or not within reach of the pet macaws.

- Ceiling fans can cause serious injury to flying birds. Surprisingly, injuries from this occur much more frequently than anyone would imagine.

- Birds do have sensitive hearing so loud noises can cause stress, leading to lowered resistance to infection or emotional problems such as feather plucking.

- Attacks by other pets in a household are a very frequent cause of injury for pet birds. Pets relish the attention of their owners so sometimes jealousy can motivate them to attack one another.

- Hot food and hot stovetops can be dangerous. Remember, even though a burner is turned off, it still remains hot enough to blister the feet of a bird for some time. A good rule is to keep the bird away from the range while there is cooking going on.

- Keep items with any chemicals away from the cage. Birds are particularly sensitive to many chemicals due to their small size and very efficient metabolism.

- Lead poisoning is one of the most common poisonings in avian practice. Due to their curiosity, birds will pick up objects, chew and occasionally swallow small fragments. Lead is absorbed into the bloodstream from the digestive tract. It is then carried to the brain and also incorporated into the bones. It can cause nervous system disorders and eventually lead to death. The diagnosis of lead poisoning is through the detection of lead in the digestive tract. If lead poisoning is suspected, veterinary assistance should be provided immediately. Radiographs will confirm the diagnosis. Blood lead analysis will confirm the diagnosis but results may take several days.

Lead poisoning can be treated if identified quickly. Calcium EDTA is the drug of choice and is given by injection into the muscle. It combines (chelates) with the lead in the bloodstream so that it cannot enter the brain. It is given until there is no evidence of lead in the GI tract or when clinical signs resolve. Mineral oil or peanut butter can be given to aid in the passage of the lead out of the GI tract. Penacillamine can also be used as a treatment for long-term therapy, an advantage being that it can be given orally.

- Houseplants can be a problem, as birds tend to nibble at vegetation, however actual plant intoxications in pet birds are quite rare. The local poison control center can provide information as to the toxicity of certain houseplants in the home. Veterinary care should be sought if there is a suspicion that a bird may have ingested a potentially toxic plant.

- Birds have the most efficient respiratory tract in the animal world. They are able to efficiently remove oxygen from the atmosphere and into the bloodstream. However, due to this efficiency and their small size, they are more sensitive to toxic elements in the air. Remember that canaries were used in mines to detect gases that would otherwise be undetectable.

- Understand Teflon toxicity. This has been a problem that I have been addressing for the past several years, having written many articles and giving numerous lectures on its danger.

  Polytetrafluoroethylene, abbreviated as (PTFE), is a hydrocarbon material or polymerization process product with heavy commercial production for use on non-stick cooking surfaces. The most familiar PTFE coated cookware is marketed under the trade names Teflon, Silverstone and Supra. However, other PTFE coated products are available under other trade names

4. They can be really noisy

If you do not like any noise in your home, then a macaw is not the best pet for you. Blue and Gold Macaws are extremely vocal birds. However, this is also a great way to communicate with your birds and understand them better.

Dealing with noisy birds

It is a natural thing for your Blue and Gold Macaw to scream for a few minutes at dawn or dusk. This is their natural way of calling out the flock.

While this behavior is acceptable, screaming becomes an issue when it is persistent.

If you notice that your bird is screaming every time you leave him alone, he is only doing this for your attention. The more attention you give him when he screams, the more he is likely to continue the behavior.

When your bird screams, leave the room without any response. If you shout back, he will believe that you are having a conversation with him. This will make him scream even louder.

Come back to your bird only when he is calm. That will help him understand that you will only go to him when he is well behaved. Keeping your parrot mentally stimulated will curb this issue to a large extent.

Whenever you leave the bird alone, give him a foraging toy or even a puzzle toy. That will make him independent and less anxious when he is all by himself.

Understanding the body language of macaws
Macaws use postures to communicate the way they are feeling. You can easily tell whether your bird is happy, angry, bored, tired or unwell just by looking at the posture. Here are a few body language tips that every Blue and Gold Macaw owner must know about:

The body

- If your bird is on your shoulder and is constantly tugging on the collar of your shirt, it means that he wants to get off.

- If the head of the bird is lowered while the wings are lifted slightly, he wants you to pick him up.

- If the bird is hanging with one or both feet from the cage, he is in a playful mood.

- If his rear end rubs the table while he walks back, he is going to take a poop.

The eyes

- All parrots exhibit pinning, which is rapid dilation of the pupils. This is either done when the bird is excited or when the bird is afraid. You can study the situation to tell how your bird is feeling.

The voice

- If the bird is talking, whistling or singing, it means that he is happy and quite content.

- If he is mumbling to himself or is just chattering softly, he is practicing the words that he learnt.

- Loud chatter is considered attention-seeking behavior.

- Clicking of the tongue means that the bird is just entertaining himself or is calling you to play with him.

- Growling is a sign of aggression. There could be something in the room that is bothering him. Removing that object will make him stop immediately.

The beak

- If you notice your bird grinding his beak just before he sleeps, it means that he is very happy to be in your home.

- Clicking of the beak when you pass by is your bird's way of greeting you. At the same time, clicking when you are holding him means that he does not want to be handled by you at the moment.

- If the beak is on the ground and the feathers are fluffed, he wants you to pet him.

- If your macaw regurgitates, it is a sign of great affection. They do this only for their mates in the wild.

- Bobbing the head is a type of attention-seeking behavior.

- If the bird is just rubbing his beak on the perch, he is cleaning himself.

Feet and legs

- If your bird is standing upright with his weight equally on both feet, he is content and happy.

- If the posture of the bird is upright and he is looking at you, it means that he wants you to pick him up right that instant.

- If the bird is feeling restless and impatient, he will rock back and forth on the perch.

- If the bird is standing on one foot, he is relaxed.

- If he is standing on foot with all his feathers fluffed, he is happy.

- If your bird is standing on one foot and has the beak tucked beneath the wing, he is just cleaning himself.

- If he is standing on one foot but is grinding his beak, he is tired.

- If he is standing on one foot with glazed eyes and semi-fluffed feathers, it means that he is falling asleep.

- If the bird is scratching the bottom of the cage, he wants you to let him out.

- Tapping of the feet indicates that the bird is trying to protect his or her territory.

The feathers

Ruffled feathers can mean one of the following things:
- The bird is feeling too cold and is trying to warm himself up.

- The bird is trying to relieve tension and stress.

- The bird is sick.

Position of the crest

- If the crest is lifted, the bird is excited.

- If the crest is puffed up it is seen as a sign of aggression.

- If the crest is flat on the ground while the bird is hissing, it means that he is scared or just getting ready to attack someone.

The tail

- If the tail is shaking, the bird is preparing for some fun time ahead.

- Tail bobbing means that the bird is tired or is catching his breath after strenuous physical activity. If this behavior is seen even when the bird has not done anything physically demanding, you need to take him to a vet immediately.

- Fanning of the tail is usually a sign of aggression. The bird is displaying his strength through this body language.

Wings

- Flapping of the wings is an attention-seeking behavior.

- Flipping of the wings could indicate one or more of the following:
- Pain or discomfort
- Anger and aggression
- A call for your attention.

- If the wings of your bird are drooping it is generally a sign that the bird is unwell.

The head

- If the head is turned back and tucked below the wing, your bird is asleep.

- When the head is lowered and turned, your bird finds something very interesting.

- If the head is down and the wings are extended, your bird is just stretching or yawning.

These simple behavior patterns will help you choose the best time to form that bond with your beloved macaw. Responding aptly to this body language also helps the bird trust you more because you are one of his own now.

5. They may develop behavioral issues

Without proper care and good mental stimulation, there are chances that your bird will develop severe behavioral issues. If you have rescued or adopted a bird, you need to be prepared for this from the beginning.

If you are not experienced with birds, it is best that you bring home a smaller bird to avoid any risks. You also have the option of hiring an experienced trainer if your bird develops the following issues:

Feather Plucking

Feather plucking is common in birds, as they use the beak to groom and preen themselves often. The only time it becomes a serious issue is when the bird is actually mutilating himself in the process of plucking the feathers out. The more frequent the feather plucking, the higher the chances of the bird injuring himself. Although it is commonly seen as a behavioral problem, there are several reasons why birds begin to pluck their own feathers, such as:

- Malnutrition
- Cysts on the skin
- Parasitic infections
- Stress
- Boredom
- Cancer
- Liver disease
- Allergies to food or dust
- Inflammation of the skin

- Skin infection
- Heavy metal poisoning
- Metabolic problems
- Dryness in the skin
- Low humidity
- Lack of proper sunlight
- Any disturbance in sleep patterns
- Presence of preservatives or dyes in the food.

A bird that has the problem of feather plucking will be rather aggressive and anxious. This may be very different from the normal demeanor of your beloved bird.

Most often, birds will suddenly display feather plucking when they are ready to breed and nest.
-
This is also called brood patch plucking. You know that your bird is plucking due to the breeding instinct because the feathers from the abdominal region and the chest area are plucked out. This is actually done by females to be able to transfer heat during the incubation phase. If your bird is not mated, sexual urges make them pluck their feathers, as they are unable to fulfill this need. Now, if your Blue and Gold Macaw is bonded with only one person in the house, it is possible that the bird thinks of that person as the mate. When the bird's "mate" showers attention on someone else, say another pet or a new baby, feather plucking is observed.

If your bird is housed in a cage that is too small or if the perch is not comfortable, he may begin to pluck his feathers out. This is because he probably feels uncomfortable and unhappy in his space. If your bird is unable to get enough exercise or mental stimulation, he will chew on his own feathers in an attempt to keep himself entertained.

If you have trimmed the wings of your bird incorrectly, he will begin to pluck his feathers as an attempt to make the feathers more even. Blue and Gold Macaws are very sensitive creatures. If they see a lot of emotional turmoil in their home such as constant fighting, they tend to develop anxiety. If they see a strange bird or cat outside a window and have got frightened. Even the smallest change in the environment such as the flickering of a light can irritate the bird enough to cause feather plucking.

This can be a really frustrating time for you as well as the bird, and he may develop habits like chewing, biting, over preening, etc. In order to curb this issue you need to be extremely patient with your bird and first get to the root of the problem. Understand why the bird is behaving in this manner. If you are unable to figure that out for yourself, you can also visit the vet for a consultation. There are some measures that you can take to help alleviate this issue:

- Keep your bird mentally stimulated.

- If he is plucking for attention, make sure that you do not give in to it. Instead, give him an out time when he starts plucking to tell him that plucking does not get your attention.

- Make sure that the food you give your bird is healthy and adequate.

- Get the feathers clipped by a professional.

- Make sure you have regular health checkups for your bird.

- The day and night lighting should be consistent. If your bird is in a room that has a TV, you might want to give him a sleeping tent so that he can get enough rest.

The problem with feather plucking is that it is not easy to fix. Your bird will always have a tendency to pluck once he begins. In addition, the rate of feather plucking and the duration depends on the cause. For example, if it is because of an infection, you can give him medicines and feather plucking will subside eventually. However, if feather plucking occurs after you got married and your bird is jealous of your spouse, it may take a lot of time for him to give this habit up. On your part, you need to be patient. If you feel like you are unable to help your bird, you can look for assistance from you avian vet. Follow all the instructions precisely and it is possible that your bird will recover soon. The best remedy for feather plucking is preventive care and ensuring that your bird is always healthy and happy.

Aggressive behavior
Aggression in Blue and Gold Macaws is usually an attempt to seek your attention. An aggressive bird will mostly display this aggression by biting. Now, what the bird really wants is your attention. If you scream or shout back at the bird, he will read it as a response. Although it is hard to not scream after a bite from the powerful mandibles of the Blue and Gold Macaw, it is necessary to keep your calm.

If the bird is perched on your body while displaying the aggressive behavior, you can do two things. First, put the bird back in the cage and ignore him until he calms down. Go to him only when he is relaxed and does not attack upon handling.

The next thing to do would be to run while the bird is perched on you. They will feel unsteady and they really dislike this feeling. If you do this every time your bird bites or nibbles at you, he will make an association with the unpleasant feeling and will eventually stop.

If aggressive behavior is a sudden manifestation, then you need to consult your vet. There are chances that the bird is in heat or has some health issue that is making him or her behave in this manner. Spending time with your bird and giving him a lot of attention will also reduce aggressive behavior.

6. They need a good amount of mental stimulus
A pet macaw requires just as much attention as a pet dog or a cat. In fact, they need a lot more mental stimulation because they are highly intelligent creatures. Without this, they are at risk of developing serious health issues.

Here are a few tips to help you keep the bird mentally stimulated. You could even come up with other activities along the way as you get to know your feathered friend's preferences and dislikes:

- Make sure that your bird has a large enough cage that he can move around freely in. If the place is too congested and small, he will just stay on the perch and will become highly inactive.

- Blue and Gold Macaws are highly social creatures. If you keep your bird in a quiet room that is completely away from the daily activities in your household, he will demand attention. Instead, make sure that this room is quiet but is facing the room with maximum activity such as the living room to help observe and stay alert at all times.

- You can introduce a companion to your bird or just buy the macaws in pairs. This works wonderfully as it keeps your bird engaged and will make him demand for your time and attention a lot less than you expect. If you are introducing the new companion, make sure you follow all the steps mentioned above to keep your bird and the new bird safe.

- Give your macaw a lot of free time. They cannot spend the whole day confined in the cage now, can they? It is advised that you give your parrot at least two hours outside the cage every day. If you have a play top cage, it will become your bird's favorite resting spot. You can even get a large parrot gym that will allow your parrot to climb and perform several acrobatics for you.

- Bring home as many bird toys as you can. You have several colors, sizes and shapes of toys that your macaw will fall in love with. Keep recycling the toys instead of throwing everything in at once. That will help you keep his interest in these toys for longer. In addition, try homemade toys like wrapping a few seeds in paper, rolling it up into a ball and placing it in the cage. See the frenzy with which your bird will attack that ball of paper.

- Include your bird in all celebrations. If you are celebrating a birthday, give the bird a few extra treats. On special occasions like Christmas or Thanksgiving, include a few gifts for your macaw as well. It is so simple to please them. All they need is a new perch or a new toy and they are good to go! This makes them feel like they are a part of some important flock ritual and will make their little hearts swell with joy.

- While you are away doing your chores or when you out to pick up groceries, you could leave the radio or TV on for your bird. This additionally helps them pick up new words and sentences. Since Blue and Gold Macaws are good speakers, they will pick up several words. The best shows for birds are cartoon shows as they are loud, cheerful, colorful and have loads of action. Giving your bird a foraging toy is the best thing to do while you are away.

Of course, you need to spend a lot of time with your bird too. Talk to him and make him feel like a part of your family. Once he is acquainted with the family, you can even keep him in the living room while you all enjoy a good movie.

Blue and Gold Macaws love to cuddle and will do just about anything for those few extra minutes on your lap or shoulder.

Training
Training is a great way to teach your bird acceptable behavior. It also keeps them stimulated and helps you bond with them.

Step up training
Step up training is the best display of trust towards the owner. Now, not only does the step up training form the basis of building the relationship, it is also one of the most important things to teach your Blue and Gold Macaw. In the case of any emergency such as a fire or a natural disaster,

you should be able to reach in and have the bird step up on your finger in order to escape. If you do not train the bird to step up, he may not let you handle him and pet him either. That makes it very difficult to do the other fun things like teaching him tricks and generally including him in various activities throughout your day.

Your hands are very scary for a new Blue and Gold Macaw. In addition, their cage is their home. When you just intrude and put your hands through, you will likely get bitten, so take it as slow as you possibly can. You will need a lot of treats that you can feed them with your hands if they are comfortable or with a spoon or a stick. When you have successfully taught your Blue and Gold Macaw to come out of the cage, you are ready to have them step up onto your finger.

The first thing to do would be to lead them to the open door of the cage. Then, you can offer your finger like a perch just a few centimeters away from the door. Remember to hold the finger horizontally so that it looks like a branch and do not point at the bird in such a way that your fingers look like food to them.

Then, hold the treat behind the perch finger. At this point, they may immediately step up or may hesitate. Do not stress them too much. Offer the step up command about two to three times and if the bird only looks at the treat and does not come for it, put the treat back in the food bowl and try again.

It is also possible that your bird will put his beak around your perch finger and gently nibble. They are not biting and you must ever draw your hand back. In the wild, birds do this to make sure that the perch is steady. So, if your bird bites your finger and you hold it still, he will probably step up, but if you draw the finger away, he will lose trust in your finger.

When he climbs up, offer him a treat. Let him stay for a while and put him back in the cage. Offer him a final treat before closing the cage door. Keep doing this for a few days. Place your perch finger, say "step up" and when he does, offer a treat. At one point just the step up command without the treat is good enough. Remember to praise your bird abundantly irrespective of whether he makes progress or not.

After you have taught the bird to step up on your finger, you can offer your shoulder as the next step. You will do the same thing; hold the bird up to your shoulder and when he steps on to it, offer him a treat. That way you can lead him up to your head as well. Getting the bird on your shoulder is great progress as it allows you to include him in all your daily activities. You can keep him on your shoulder as you fold laundry, do the dishes or even just sit down and read a book. That way, he will feel like you are giving him attention and is likely to bond faster.

Once you have established the trust to get the Blue and Gold Macaw to step up on to your finger, you can try to pet him. Start by stroking the head and the cheeks. If he allows you to do that, you can move on to the critical part, which is touching the beak. If your Blue and Gold Macaw allows you to touch the beak without biting, then it means that he has established a high level of trust in you.

When you are teaching the Blue and Gold Macaw anything new, whether he is learning to come out of the cage or on to your finger, you need to spend at least 15 minutes everyday. You need to keep the time of training and the place of training consistent for better results.

Toilet training
When you are taking your bird all over the house with you after step up training, the last thing you want is your furniture and carpet to be covered with poop. You need to tell your bird that he can poop only in an assigned place and not anywhere else in the house. The first step is to help him understand that his cage is a good place to do his business.

You can start doing this with the first poop of the day. In the morning, when you are feeding the bird and cleaning up the bowls, place a fresh newspaper under the perch and wait for the bird to poop. Watch his body language when he does this. Knowing the changes in the body is very useful in further training. When he poops, praise him and give him a treat. That tells him that pooping in the cage is a good thing.

Usually, when birds poop, they tend to crunch their bodies and hold it stiff. Other birds may have other changes in the body language. When you begin to step the bird up and walk around your home with him, watch out for these signs. The moment you see this you can put a tissue under the bird and let him go about his business. When he does poop on the paper, praise him. If he poops elsewhere, don't react. No reaction is worse than reprimanding for a bird.

He will eventually learn that pooping on paper is good. You can then step the training up and hold the paper over a bin or inside the cage. When the bird uses this designated place, praise him and give him a treat. He will slowly understand that every time he needs to poop, he will have to go to the bin or to the cage in order to keep you happy.

Birds as large as the Blue and Gold Macaw will poop every 20 minutes at least. This means that there are chances of accidents. Be patient and do not reprimand the bird unnecessarily. Instead, until your bird is fully potty trained, keep the expensive carpets and rugs away.

7. They can be a threat to children and other pets

While Blue and Gold Macaws are friendly for the most part, they are easily threatened or spooked. This leads to a quick nip or even a bite sometimes. The sheer power and size of the beak of these birds can be very dangerous to children, other birds in the house or even other household pets. The key is to make sure that you set ground rules and also ensure that they are introduced properly to avoid any accidents and mishaps.

How to introduce Blue and Gold Macaws to kids

If you have a newborn baby in your home, it is advised that you do not bring home a Blue and Gold Macaw. They both require a lot of attention. If you are unable to give the bird the attention he needs, he may grow jealous of the baby and may even attack the child.

Now, if you already have a Blue and Gold Macaw and then have a baby, never go to the bird only after the baby is put away in the crib. Then the Blue and Gold Macaw gets a message that he is loved only when the baby is away. That leads to jealousy and anger. Such a bird will attack the baby or may start exhibiting behavior such as feather plucking. Make sure that you go about your daily routine with the bird while the baby is in the room. It is not a good idea to let the bird out of the cage, though.

If you want to bring a Blue and Gold Macaw home to teach your child responsibility, you must wait until the child is older. This is a good pet for pre-teens or teenagers. If you have a little one at home who is younger than 7 years of age, it is not advisable to leave him/her alone with the bird.

These birds have hooked beaks. That is something you must never underestimate. These beaks are strong and sharp and can inflict serious damage upon anyone. Most often birds like Blue and Gold Macaws that are social will be kind and gentle towards everyone in the family, but if you cross a line, he will let you know. Now with a child who is less than 7 years of age this could happen by accident, leading to serious injuries.

It is a rule of the thumb that larger parrots are easier to form relationships with. So, if you have had a budgie or a cockatiel, it is not the same as having a Blue and Gold Macaw. These birds need a lot more work to turn them into great companions. If you are patient enough, you will have a friend for life. Even if you are a first time owner or if you have a child in your home that wants a Blue and Gold Macaw, you can both build very successful relationships with the bird if you are willing to learn and be patient with him. A child must not be allowed to do this unsupervised.

Children tend to get scared easily and may react with a scream when the bird is being playful. In some cases, children could just get naughty and tease the bird. Both these situations are negative for your parrot and he will react by either nipping or attacking the child. The bird is not to be blamed, as he/she is only responding by instinct. You cannot blame the child because, well, it is a child. As an adult, you need to be very responsible about introducing your bird to the child at the appropriate age.

How to introduce Blue and Gold Macaws to other birds
The first step to introducing new birds is to have the bird quarantined for 30 days at least. This gives you enough time to observe the bird for any signs of infection that could be contagious. To quarantine the new bird, you need to keep him or her in a separate cage, in a separate room. Birds will get acquainted with one another thanks to their loud calls. So, you can expect your pet birds to be ready for a new member during the introduction.

It is never a good idea to place birds of different sizes in the same cage. The larger bird might become more dominating, putting the smaller bird at great risk. If you have an aviary with birds about the same size as the Blue and Gold Macaws such as the Cockatoo, you could keep them together. However, there is no guarantee that your birds will be friendly with each other and will take to each other's company.

During the actual introduction, you will introduce your Blue and Gold Macaw to the least dominant bird in the flock. You can first start by placing them in separate cages side by side. You can also get a new cage that they both can be placed in, in order to reduce territorial behavior. If the birds just mind their own business and do not attack one another, you can consider it a successful introduction. You can progress to the more dominant birds in the same fashion.

These introductions will only happen in your presence so that you can observe the behavior of the birds. When you are introducing the more dominant birds to your Blue and Gold Macaw, it is best to do it in a more open space like the living room. This gives the bird ample room to run away or fly away if there is any sign of aggression from the other one.

After you are certain that these individual introductions went well, you can place the bird in the aviary. Watch the reaction of the other birds carefully. If you notice that one of them retreats completely, it is a sign that he or she is not happy with the new member in the group. On the other hand, if you see your Blue and Gold Macaw being chased around the cage, he could be in danger of attacks and wounds.

Birds may get along with no traces of jealousy or dominance at times, but if this does not happen in your home despite several attempts, it is not a matter of great disappointment. Sometimes, birds may just not get along with one another. That is when you place them in separate cages and leave them alone.

This ensures that no bird is harmed unnecessarily. You will also prevent a great deal of stress that the bird may go through when he is introduced to another bird who is so hostile or even aggressive in some cases.

How to introduce Blue and Gold Macaws to other pets

Most pet owners are often in a dilemma whether they can bring a parrot into a home with a pet like a cat or a dog. On the one hand, you see so many online videos of birds and dogs being wonderful companions and on the other hand you cannot help but think about the instinctive behavior of these animals.

Well, instinct always wins. You see, in the wild, these animals are predators of the Blue and Gold Macaws or any other bird. So, the bird may view them as a threat and initiate the attack. Now, even if the gentlest dog accidentally gets his mouth around the bird, it is certainly dangerous.

With cats, you need to be more careful, as they are curious creatures. They will try to climb the cage of your bird just to figure out who this new member in the family is. This curious meeting may go wrong, potentially injuring the bird and the cat. The bird is at a greater risk because the saliva of the cat is fatal to the bird.

Therefore, before you introduce your pet to your bird, you need to weigh up all the possible interactions. However, it is certain that you need to make them aware of each other's presence. When the bird is acclimatized to your home and has settled in, you can place the cage of the bird where the dog or the cat spends most of his time.

Initially, your pet will be extremely curious and will try to sniff the cage and even be a little restless around the new creature. If the dog barks or growls, take the bird away. If the cat tries to climb on the cage, discourage that immediately.

Both behaviors are threatening for the bird and will reduce any chances of getting along in the future. Maintain these enclosed interactions until the pets do not react to the presence of your bird. The next question is whether you can let your bird out of the cage or not.

If your bird is not capable of flight, it is probably too much of a risk. In case the pet gets too excited and approaches the bird, he may not be able to get away to safety. Otherwise, you can try supervised interactions outside the cage while holding your dog or cat. If the latter gets too edgy and aggressive, you may not want to encourage these out of cage interactions.

In any case, make sure that your bird is in the cage and the pets are in their enclosure when you leave the house. They should not be able to have accidental encounters that may lead to untoward incidents. Sometimes, these unsupervised interactions may turn out to be great and sometimes, it could lead to serious injuries for both animals. The risk is too high and so, it is best that you avoid them.

8. They do not warm up to you instantly

It is true that Blue and Gold Macaws love to cuddle and play with their owners. However, this requires you to take some time to build trust with your bird. Only when you have formed a bond and understood how to handle the bird should you approach him. To begin with, it is best that you let the bird get used to your home and his new environment.

Following this, you can start with slow interactions and work your way up.

How to introduce the macaw into your home

The experience of being transferred from the pet store to a new home is not just difficult, but actually traumatic for Blue and Gold Macaws. So it is best to leave them alone for a while. Especially when you are driving home, do not talk to the parrot. Your voice is new to them and too alien, so their stress just goes up tenfold.

Once you are home, open the enclosure, place the opening of the box or the carrier towards the opening of the enclosure and just wait for your bird to walk into his new home. This will take a few minutes. In addition, this is when you will understand why a cat carrier or a smaller cage is a better option than a box in order to transfer the Blue and Gold Macaw.

Gently close the door of the enclosure and just leave your Blue and Gold Macaw alone. Do not talk, tap the cage or just sit and stare at the bird. It is stressful for him. Instead, go about your routine, but do not leave your house. He should be able to see you in the new environment. Therefore, it is a good idea to choose a first day for the parrot when you are going to be home all day.

If you have a hand-bred bird, it is safe to interact with them after a few hours. Even this should be very gentle. You can place your hands on the sides of the bird's enclosure and just let him explore. He may come and taste your finger. If he allows you to, stroke his cheeks and head with your finger. That way he knows that you are safe to approach. Then, you can say hello in a very soft voice. Keep the conversation on the first day limited and your bird will be able to cope.

Ask the breeder or the pet store owner for the favorite treat of your bird. Keeping this handy will actually help you reduce the stress of the Blue and Gold Macaw to a large extent. If you do not have bird food already, you can purchase some from your breeder or the pet store. This is the only preparation that you need to make for the first day.

If your Blue and Gold Macaw is aviary bird, it is best to leave him alone for at least two days. Your interaction should be limited to the feeding time. Remember that you never want to establish any dominance or submission with Blue and Gold Macaws. This can be done by maintaining your eyes at the eye level of the Blue and Gold Macaw every time you interact. Crouch down or step on a stool if you have to. That way you tell the bird that you are a friend or an equal.

How to establish trust with macaws
For the next week, try to talk as little as you can to your parrot. Keep socialization to a minimum. This means that you will not host parties or have people over for at least one week after the parrot arrives. You also need to keep noises like the TV and radio at a minimum.

Make sure you pass by the cage often. That way, your bird will get accustomed to your presence. You will also be interacting with the bird when you are feeding him and cleaning the cage. This is the bonding time.

After a day or two, you can say words like "Hello" and "Bye" in a very soft and soothing voice. With a Blue and Gold Macaw, do not be surprised if he responds with the same words.

Once you think that the bird is ready, you can start actual interaction. You will know that your bird is ready by observing his body language. His posture will be erect. He will use the perch. His level of activity will increase. In addition, when you approach the cage to feed him, he will not cover himself or retreat behind the towel. That indicates that your bird is getting used to your home. With Blue and Gold Macaws, this will happen much faster than any other parrot species because they are naturally very social creatures.

Now you can sit by the cage and talk to your bird in a calm voice. Just place your hands on the wall of the cage for a while and sit in front of the cage quietly. The bird will approach your hand, lick it and probably even nibble at it. This is a good sign, as it shows that your bird is not afraid of you. You can even move your hand around the walls and see if the bird follows your hand. If he does, then he is warming up to you.

When you are interacting with your bird, make sure that you are at his eye level at all times. When you are feeding, cleaning or even just talking to him, stay at the same level as him. If you tower over the cage, he will view you as a predator and will get scared of you. He will also assume that you mean harm if he feels like you are much larger than him in size.

Staying at eye level, on the other hand, tells him that you are part of his flock and that you are both equals in the group. This will help him trust you more and approach you more positively.

The first thing you want to accomplish with your bird is trust. This is a slow process but once you have managed it, it can be extremely rewarding. Start by just spending a few minutes every day, talking to the bird and just placing your hand on the walls of the enclosure.

If you are the one feeding him every day, he is likely to bond faster. If your bird begins to respond by approaching your hand, licking it or nibbling at it slowly, it is a good sign. You can then start offering treats through the bars of the cage. If your bird does not eat it, just leave it in the cage and keep trying. Once the bird accepts a treat from your hand, the next step is to let him out of the cage.

Just open the cage door and let the bird come out. He will probably climb up on the cage and just explore the space around. Make sure that the space is safe for your bird and free from threats like pets or ceiling fans.

Then, you can hold out some treats in your hand and see if the bird will approach your hand. When your bird starts eating comfortably from your hand, it means that he is tamed enough to start the actual training.

Putting the bird back is easy. Just leave a few of his favorite treats or toys in the cage and he will go to them. In case your bird is reluctant to go into the cage before he is hand tamed, use toweling to handle him. Wrap his body in a thick towel and let the ends fall over your hand. Then, pick him up gently holding the wings down and put him back in the cage. Treats and toys will help him understand that the cage is a fun place to be in.

9. There may be legal considerations
In a nutshell, the laws guiding the permits and conditions of keeping macaws are quite flexible. By flexible, the reference is to the provision of optimal rights of both the human and the creatures involved.

The question as to whether it is legal or not to own a macaw is relative. It all comes down to which state you live in.

There are some states that are opposed to owning macaws, other are for it. Therefore, ensure that you do some background checked with the state legal departments to be in line with their minimum requirements When a macaw lover crosses a state or national border, they should be wary of the regulations about the ownership of birds and pets in general. The requirements will range from nothing to as stringent as even specifying the cage size.

The legalities of owning a macaw in particular may lead to numerous legal tussles. What should one do if their neighbor sues them for nuisance if the macaw is rather noisy? You should consider all of this before getting one.

When it comes to the transit of the birds, the state departments control the licensing and permits for the transit itself. The goal is to maintain ultimate control on the movement of the birds. A reasonable instance is in the outbreak of air-borne diseases. The state departments are authorized to license when an outbreak is put under full control. This is for the interest of both the macaw and its owner. This provides a win-win scenario for everyone involved

10. They are a steady financial commitment

Macaws are a big financial responsibility. Therefore, you need to be sure that you can sustain the costs involved. You should have enough funds available to take care of the bird for a good 30 years at least. Here is a break-up of the cost of owning a Blue and Gold Macaw.

The most important part of raising your parrot. The minimum expenses include:

- Cost of the bird: If you decide to adopt a Blue and Gold Macaw, it will cost you approximately $150 or £75. If you buy a bird from a breeder or a pet store, it will cost you about $650-100 or £350-800.

- Cost of the cage: You must never compromise on the quality of the cage and ensure that your bird gets nothing but the best. A good cage will cost you about $180-400 or £100-200. It should be made from good material and should be secure for the bird.

- Food expenses: It is necessary to give your parrot a good mixture of fresh produce and pellets. Of course, you need to add treats as well. If you add up all the costs, it will come up to at least $50 or £30 each month.

- Veterinary costs: Veterinary costs will go up to $1200 or £800 annually. On an average, every consultation should cost you close to $50 or £30.

- Toys: You need to keep buying new toys to keep a Blue and Gold Macaw entertained. You can expect to spend at least $30 or £15 each month on the toys alone.

- Insurance: As discussed before, insurance can cost up to $250 or £150 each month depending upon the coverage that you opt for.

On average, you could spend close to $400 or £200 each month on bird care. Before you bring a bird home, make sure that you take this sum out of your monthly income and put it away. If you are able to manage all your expenses for the month and if you can keep this up for at least three months, you are ready for the financial commitment of a Blue and Gold Macaw. If not you may have to wait a little longer or figure out how you will manage these expenses.

Chapter 3: Where to Buy your Blue and Gold Macaw

Finding the right source for your Blue and Gold macaw will make all the difference. You have the option of buying from a breeder or a pet store or adopting a bird.

The goal is to make sure that you bring home a healthy bird. If not, you will have to bear additional costs of veterinary care. If the bird is extremely sick, it can be fatal as well. In addition to that, there are some diseases that can affect humans as well.

Making sure that your source is genuine and uses ethical commercial procedure is vital before you buy a bird from it.

1. Buying from a breeder

There are several Blue and Gold Macaw Breeders in all the areas where these birds are popular pets. You can find a breeder near your home by looking up websites like www.birdbreeders.com that carry listings of some of the most popular breeders in your locality. If you are not one who relies on Internet searches, you can even ask a bird store owner to help you find one. You can even speak to fellow Blue and Gold Macaw owners to introduce you to the breeders that they work with.

The advantage of getting your birds from a breeder is that they are likely to be healthier. You see, most breeders will focus on one type or family of birds. They will spend a lot of time learning about them and putting together the best breeding practices to produce healthy babies. You have various scales at which people practice Blue and Gold Macaw breeding. Some of them just have a backyard breeding business and others choose to do this on a more professional level. Either way, you should be able to find a healthy bird if you find a good breeder.

Now, you have several breeders who will sell these birds through online stores. That is acceptable only if you are certain about the reputation of the breeder. Otherwise, it is recommended that you pay at least one visit to the facility to check out the breeding conditions. There is one rule of thumb when it comes to breeders: if the environment is clean, the birds will be healthy. Check how the cages have been maintained, see if there is clean water for the birds and also understand how much these breeders actually interact with their birds. That way you can be certain of not just a healthy bird but also one that is social to some extent. Here are some handy tips when you are choosing a breeder to buy your bird from:

- Check for their experience. It is mostly suggested that you opt for breeders who have been in the business for a good amount of time. They will have experience with respect to various issues faced by bird owners and will become a valuable source of support for new bird owners. Of course, there may be some new breeders who are extremely passionate about their birds. In such cases, check for how much experience they have with managing and handling Blue and Gold Macaws, be it their own pets or pets of friends and family.

- Check if they have an avian veterinarian. This is very critical. Every good breeder will be associated with an avian veterinarian. That is how they are able to have the birds regularly examined to give you some guarantee on their health. If the breeder does not have an avian veterinarian that he or she can recommend, you may want to look for new options immediately.

- The breeder must follow the closed aviary concept. That way you can be sure that the birds that come to your home will be disease free.

- Check the breeder's website. If you have come to know of a breeder through an email or a flyer, you must check for a website immediately. All good breeders will have one and will tell you in detail about their breeding practices on these websites.

- Look for recommendations. This is undoubtedly the best way to find a reliable breeder. You can ask the breeder if you can talk to other Blue and Gold Macaw owners that he or she deals with just to understand how they have been able to cope with the bird. In the process, you will know if the owner and the breeder share a good relationship or not. If the breeder is hesitant to connect you to their customers, it is a sign of something fishy.

A breeder who truly looks out for his or her birds will also be a valuable part of raising your Blue and Gold Macaw. He or she will be able to help you with all the initial preparations that you need to make in order to welcome your pet Blue and Gold Macaw home. Along with a vet, your breeder is the only support you will need to raise a healthy bird in your home.

Should you opt for a closed aviary?
This is common practice among most bird breeders to ensure that the birds are free from any diseases. They follow strict quarantining rules to prevent any germs from entering their flock and damaging the health of the birds. There are a few rules that are followed with the closed aviary:

- Usually new birds are not added to the flock: If there is a need to add a new bird for whatever reason, they make sure that it is quarantined for a minimum period of 3 months and a maximum of 6 months.

- The birds that are taken to the vet are quarantined too: Now, the chances of catching infections and diseases are maximum at the vet. So, breeders quarantine them to ensure that they do not bring back any air borne virus. Even at the vet, these birds are usually covered with large towels to reduce the risk of infections.

- They keep all birds off the premises: That means they do not allow their friends, customers or anyone bring birds in. Even rescues are not permitted unless there is a chance to quarantine them first.

- They do not go to any place where there are other birds: This includes pet stores and even bird shows. They definitely do not take their birds there. If they themselves go to one such event, they will take a shower and change their clothes fully before handling their own aviary. They do this to ensure that there are no chances of any indirect contact resulting in infections.

- Breeders with these practices can be trusted as they invest a lot of energy to keep the health of their birds at its peak.

2. Buying from a pet store
Getting a Blue and Gold Macaw from a pet store should be your last option. The reason for this is that these birds do not get the specialized care that they require when they are in a pet store with several other birds and animals, perhaps. However, if you are convinced that a local pet store is known for the quality of Blue and Gold Macaws that they sell, here are a few things that you need to keep in mind:

- Make sure that the pet store has a license to sell exotic birds. You can check the CITES website for all the details on the license required to buy and sell exotic birds.

- You need to ensure that these birds are being sourced by local breeders. Since importing these birds is illegal, these birds should be bred in captivity. Find out about the breeder that they deal with in detail.

- Check the environment that the bird is being raised in. A macaw is not a commodity that you pick off the shelf even if it is in a slightly messy environment. These birds hate crammed and dirty places. They will develop behavioral problems and could also be carriers of several diseases when kept in such conditions.

- The pet store should provide a health guarantee for the birds that they sell, especially the exotic ones. Insist on this guarantee because Blue and Gold Macaws are extremely expensive.

- The bird should look healthy and active. On the other hand, if he or she is lethargic and is afraid of people, it might be a challenge for you to make the bird a part of your family.

- The staff should be interested in the well being of the bird and should be able to provide you with information regarding the care and maintenance of the bird. If you see that they are negligent and are only trying to make a sale, they have most likely invested almost nothing in the bird's well being.

A Blue and Gold Macaw is a wonderful companion, no doubt. However, it is not the easiest bird to have in a household. If you feel like you need to learn a little more about the birds, spend time at pet stores to see how they behave and how demanding they can be.

Adoption centers would be happy to have volunteers who can take care of the birds. This is also a great idea for you to get used to these birds. Their size may be awe-inspiring. However, it is the sheer size of these birds that can make you feel like you are incompetent to take care of them. Handling them, feeding them and even just having them on your shoulder is a lot harder in comparison to a smaller bird.

You can even join local bird groups or dedicated Blue and Gold Macaw forums to learn more about the bird. Do not be too impulsive about

48

purchasing a Blue and Gold Macaw. Take your time and only make a decision when you know enough about the bird.

3. Adopting a Blue and Gold Macaw

If you are a slightly experienced bird owner, you are probably ready to adopt a Blue and Gold Macaw. What you need to know about adopting any bird is that you are probably going to find an adult bird that also has a history of abandonment or even abuse. These birds tend to be shy or aggressive depending on the experiences that they have had in the past.

With adoption, you need to know that the birds need additional care, which you will be able to provide only after you have some experience with the birds. You may also have to spend more money on the medical treatment of these birds in order to bring them back to good health. Since the Blue and Gold Macaw is also a rare species, there are several policies regarding the adoption of these birds.

Adoption agencies that work with species like the Blue and Gold Macaw are very particular about the care that the birds are going to receive. Therefore, they have two options for all the birds that come under their care. One is lifetime sanctuary where the birds are kept in the adoption center until they die. This is normally done when the bird requires that kind of attention because of some health issue that it has. In addition to that, when some people give their birds up, they request lifetime care to make sure that the bird is in good hands.

The second option is when the birds are put up for adoption. Now, with the Blue and Gold Macaw, they are exceptionally careful about the adoption process, as these birds are highly vulnerable to exploitation for commercial gains.

The adoption process

The first step to adopting a Blue and Gold Macaw is to fill in an application form for adoption. This application form will ask for details about your profession, your experience with birds and also the reason for adoption.

Following this application form, you will be asked to take basic lessons about caring for Blue and Gold Macaws. These lessons could either be online or offline. You will also be given access to a lot of their educational material that you can refer to after taking the bird home. Many adoption agencies require that you complete a certain number of these basic classes before you are allowed to take a bird home.

After you have completed the required number of training hours, you will be allowed to take a tour of the aviary and the adoption center. That way, you get an idea about all the birds that are available for adoption. There are several cases when people decide that they want a certain bird but end up getting a different species altogether.

The idea is to form a bond with the right bird. Macaws are birds with large personalities. If your personality does not match the bird's personality, you will have a tough time getting your bird to bond with you and actually want to be around you.

The last thing to do would be to visit the bird of your choice frequently. Once you have made up your mind to take a certain macaw home, you need to let the bird get acquainted with you. You will also learn simple things like handling the bird, feeding him and cleaning the cage up etc. from the experts at the adoption agency.

Sometimes, it may so happen that you set your heart and mind on one bird that just does not seem to be interested. It is natural for that to happen. All you need to do is be patient with the bird and visit him as many times as you can.

When you are ready to take the bird home, most of these adoption centers will pay a visit to your home and will take care of all the little details required to help you get the bird settled into your home.

Now, if you already have pet birds at home, you will be required to present a full veterinary test result of each bird. This helps the agency ensure that the bird they are sending to your home does not have any vulnerability to fatal diseases. There are certain health standards that each of these agencies set for the health of your pet bird.

Are there any fees involved?

Most agencies and foundations will charge you an application fee that will include access to educational DVDs, toys and other assistance from the foundation.

You will also have to pay an adoption fee that may go up to $100 or £500 for a Blue and Gold Macaw. These two separate fees are charged to make sure that you get all the assistance that you need with respect to making a positive start with your Blue and Gold Macaw.

In addition to that, most agencies charge a rather high fee to ensure that the individuals who are investing in the bird are genuinely interested in having the bird. These fees will ward off people who want to just take the bird home for free with no clue about its care. Of course, you also need to consider the care provided to these birds while they are under the care of the foundation. These fees cover all of that including the medical requirements of your bird. It is also the only source to pay the dedicated staff that take care of these abandoned or rescued birds day in and day out.

From the time you make the application for a Blue and Gold Macaw, it takes about 6-10 weeks for it to be approved and for the bird to be sent to your home. Most of these centers will also have a probationary period of 90 days during which you will have to keep sending records of how the bird is progressing to them. They will also pay home visits to ensure that the bird is being maintained well without any health issues. If the ambience or the facilities provided to the bird are not good enough, the bird will be taken back with no reimbursement of the adoption fee.

4. Is buying online a good idea?

Many pet owners believe that buying from an online breeder is actually quite a good idea. It certainly is if the breeder is well known and has a reputation for selling only healthy birds. However, with a bird as expensive as the Blue and Gold Macaw, this is not a risk that is worth taking.

You need to understand that with online breeders, you have no way of knowing how the birds have been maintained. There could be several pictures on their website, however, unless you can check the place yourself or can have a friend or family member do that for you, it is advisable not to invest in online purchases.

There is a 50% chance that you will get a beautiful, healthy bird. However the other 50% is a risk that you cannot take with Blue and Gold Macaws. Even if you pay half the price of the bird as an advance, it is a good amount of money.

With online breeders, even a reputable one is not advisable for birds like this. You see, after the bird has been shipped, there is not much control that the breeder has over the travelling conditions of the bird.

There are chances that you will get a fatigued bird whose health has been compromised due to lack of food or proper transport conditions.

If you insist on the online purchase of a Blue and Gold Macaw for convenience purposes, here are a few things that you need to keep in mind:

- Only opt for breeders who can be recommended by friends and family. They should have personally made a purchase for the recommendation to be of value to you.

- Do not choose a breeder that is too far away from your city. It is best to choose someone in a city that you can reach in under 5 hours by flight. If your birds need to spend long hours on the flight, it is not good for his health.

- Ask for a health certificate with your bird. Tests should be based on blood and fecal samples. That helps you ensure that there are no chances of psittacosis in your Blue and Gold Macaw.

- Ask your breeders to provide you with contacts of people that he/she has shipped birds to in the past. Any good breeder will share this information easily.

Of course, with online purchases, scams cannot be neglected. There are several individuals who will try to make a quick buck out of your requirements.

There have been instances when potential owners have received pictures of birds that belong to someone else.

You can catch a scam pretty easily. They will approach you persistently to make a sale. In addition to that, they will ask you to pay small amounts in intervals. They will keep on adding new expenses like insurance, transport, etc. An authorized breeder will know what expenses are involved and will give you a full invoice and costing for transporting the bird.

When a breeder approaches you to make a sale, make sure you ask them questions about Blue and Gold Macaws. Ask them about the breeding season of the bird, the diet, the care required, etc. These questions should be asked over the phone to make sure that they are not looking for answers online.

Anyone interested in just scamming you will have no idea about these birds most often.

Lastly, you need to ask them for contacts of people that they have already sold birds to. If they are reluctant or do not share this information for any other reason, you need to become aware that they are trying to scam you.

People have lost hundreds of dollars trying to make online purchases. Most of these websites will be pulled down within days of "making a sale" or getting an advance from people. Remember, never pay the full amount to a breeder until you receive the bird in good condition when you are placing an order online.

5. How to check if a bird is healthy

If you see the following at a pet store or the breeder's, you need to make sure that you start looking for other options immediately:

- **The cage is unclean:** If the cage is poorly maintained, it is a definite red flag. You will notice feathers stuck to the grill. If there is dried poop on the floor of the cage, it means that the cage is not cleaned on a regular basis. The water bowl should have clean water. If you notice droppings in the food bowl or the water bowl, it means that the birds are not well maintained. Any good pet store or breeder will know that most avian diseases are spread due to unclean conditions that the birds grow in. They will try to maintain the best standards as far as sanitation and cage maintenance are concerned.

- **The bird is only given seeds:** There are two important reasons why you must avoid a breeder or pet store that only gives the birds seeds. First, it is very difficult to change the diet of your bird to a healthier one. Second, birds that eat only seeds may have severe nutritional deficiencies that can make the bird prone to infections and several unwanted diseases. Ideally, the bird should be given a variety of foods in order to remain healthy. They must get fruits and vegetables along with pellets as part of their diet. If a peek into the food bowl is not good enough for you to understand the actual diet of the bird, you can quiz the pet store owner or the breeder.

- **The bird is not active:** Birds are always very alert. Being prey animals, this is their natural disposition. When you approach the cage, the bird should respond in some way. Their posture will become erect, they will lean in towards you to understand who you are or they will at least fly away to a hiding spot. On the other hand, if the bird is lethargic and unresponsive, it is a sign of poor health.

There are other signs that you can look for such as:

- The nares of the Blue and Gold Macaw should be dry. Nares are the Nasal cavity of the bird. If you see any mucus or wetness, it is a sign of infection.

- If you have a chance of handling the bird, feel the body. There should not be any lumps. You must especially check the underside of the wings and the belly for any such lumps.

- Typically, a Blue and Gold Macaw is stout but not plump. If you see excess weight on the body of the Blue and Gold Macaw that you choose, you need to be concerned.

- Blue and Gold Macaws are active birds. If they are lethargic or do not react immediately upon seeing you approach their cage it is a sign of some behavioral problem or some issue in the eating habits of the bird.

- Make sure that the Blue and Gold Macaw has an erect posture. That is a sign of good skeletal development, which is essential for the bird's health.

- The eyes should be clear and not puffy and watery. This is also a sign of infection.

- When you are looking at bringing a chick home, it is essential that their feathers are not damp and ruffled. This is a sign of poor sanitation and husbandry.

- Check the legs and the feet. The skin on it should look healthy.

- In the case of any bird, the beak is the first sign of health. If there is any damage to the beak or any abnormality, you need to check with a vet.

These are the first signs of health with respect to the Blue and Gold Macaws. However, the first two days of bringing the bird home are the most critical ones. This is when you will discover how healthy your bird is.

The health of the bird is the most important factor in deciding if you want to bring him home or not. Of course, you have to worry about the additional care an unwell bird will demand. It also means that the bird has not been given positive experiences in the growing years. Being in an unclean environment and not getting enough attention can be stressful for birds leading to unwanted behavioral issues like aggression or extreme fear.

6. Are handfed birds better?
If you are a first time buyer, insist on birds that have been handfed only. While it is possible to train Blue and Gold Macaws pretty easily considering their intelligence, it is not really a good idea to train the birds after you have brought them into your home if you are a first time owner.

Now, our fingers and hands are pretty intimidating to birds. They also closely resemble branches of trees or even worms to most birds. They are likely to take a bite of them or just nibble on your fingers as an attempt to find a suitable perch. With smaller birds, this is acceptable, but if you bring home a juvenile or adult Blue and Gold Macaw, even the slightest friendly nibble can cause some serious damage.

These birds have a very strong biting ability and are known to easily crack the hardest nuts with great ease. Therefore, new owners should look for birds that have been handfed.

When they are younger, hand feeding these birds makes them used to the way our hands move. These birds are comfortable being handled and are less likely to perceive your fingers as a threat. It is also much easier to train these birds.

However, if you want to hand train the birds yourself, it is a good idea to bring home a baby. These birds are smaller and their bite will not hurt you as much. Of course, with younger birds, they are not as easily threatened. They tend to be more welcoming because of their curiosity towards new experiences.

For first time owners, handfed birds are the easier and safer options. If you adopt or want to bring home an adult bird that is not hand tamed, it is a good idea to look for a professional trainer who can help you train the bird.

Chapter 4: Bonding with Blue and Gold Macaws

Spending as much time with your macaw is the key to bonding with your bird. Training and feeding are great ways to bond with your bird. However, there is more you can do to get your bird used to your presence and your touch. This will make him more inclined to you and will also love to cuddle and play with you. Here are some ideas for you to bond with your Blue and Gold Macaw.

1. Grooming

Grooming allows the bird to get used to your touch. It is also a great way for you to keep your bird healthy and clean. This is also a chance for you to examine your bird to understand if there are any abnormalities on the body or in the plumage of your bird. This is extremely useful in detecting health issues that can be detrimental. There are two important grooming activities with respect to Blue and Gold Macaws.

Bathing

Bathing a Blue and Gold Macaw is very simple. All you need to do is mist the body of the bird with a spray bottle of water. Only when you see matted feathers should you gently brush the area to remove the debris. Soap is not required to bathe your Blue and Gold Macaw unless there is a lot of debris that is stuck on the feathers of the bird.

If you do use soap, make sure that it is very mild and that it is thoroughly rinsed off the bird's body. You can even hold the bird under a warm shower. They will enjoy this, as it resembles the rain that they are so used to in the rainforests that they originate from.

If the bird turns away from the spray of water and looks uncomfortable, take him out of there immediately. A bird who is enjoying the bath will lift his feathers and turn around to soak the whole body.

Water baths are popular with all breeds of birds. Place a shallow bowl with water and slowly lower the bird into the bath. If your bird is still not hand trained, you can even put a few celery pieces in the water. As the bird forages, he will also bathe himself.

There is a certain season called the molting season when the birds shed old feathers and grow new ones. This is a very uncomfortable phase for the bird, as his skin will be highly irritable. To fix this, you can give the bird a good misting with a spray bottle. You can use water that is at room temperature to ease the discomfort.

Wing and Toenail clipping

Many people advocate against wing clipping. However, in many cases owners find it easier to manage the bird when he is not able to fly off. Blue and Gold Macaws are not stopped by cages and if the quality of the cage is not good enough, you can expect several escapes. Even when you are traveling with the bird, keeping the wings clipped is a good idea.

To clip the wings, it is best that you consult a professional if you have not done it before. It will not cost more than $10 or £5 pounds.

If you want to do this at home, it is best to wrap a towel around the bird's body. Then, let one wing out of the lose end. Cut about 1 cm from the largest feathers that are called the primary feathers. Repeat this on the opposite side and make sure that you cut the feathers equally.

If you catch a blood feather, you can stop the bleeding with flour. This will not render the bird incapable of flying but will give him lesser lift. The wings are used to balance the body as well so cutting feathers on both sides equally is a must.

To clip the toenails, just place your finger below the overgrown part of the nail and file the nail slightly. Do not make it too short as it impairs the bird's ability to climb and hold their food. The nail should only be blunt enough to make sure it does not get stuck to the upholstery around your home.

Natural grooming methods

The process by which birds keep their feathers in good shape and well groomed is called preening. With almost 25000 feathers, it is natural for a bird to want to constantly work towards each one of them to keep them in the best condition. This is a behavioral pattern that you will observe with just about any species of birds.

There is a gland called the uropygial gland that is found just below the tail of most birds. This gland releases oils that contain natural waxes that help in keeping the feathers waterproof. In addition to that, the feathers also become more flexible with the application of this oil. Each feather is protected and coated as the bird applies the secretions of this gland on each feather.

What is interesting with Blue and Gold Macaws and all parrots is that this gland is absent. Instead, the feathers are broken down into fine power that is applied on the body.

There are several advantages of preening besides making the bird look good. Some of the important benefits of preening include:

- Aligning the feathers in such a way that they keep the bird insulated and protected from water.

- The shape of the feathers is maintained in aerodynamically feasible manner to improve flight.

- Parasites and lice that carry diseases are removed to keep not just themselves but the entire flock safe.

- When the feathers molt, the bird needs to remove a tough coating that is seen on the new feathers. That way the new feathers can be kept in place.

- The bird looks healthier when preened properly and is more likely to attract a mate.

2. Traveling with your macaw

In case you plan to take your macaw on a vacation with you, or if you need to move from your current residence, it is necessary for you to follow the right methods of transporting your bird. With birds like the Blue and Gold Macaw especially, the legal considerations are another aspect of transporting your bird.

What are the legalities involved?

Almost all species of exotic birds including Blue and Gold Macaws are protected by strict rules laid out by CITES. If you are planning to travel with your Blue and Gold Macaw, you need to be sure that you are aware of all these legalities.

First, when you decide to take your bird to another country or state, you will have to check permit requirements. Some states will require a permit under the regulations of CITES while others will require you to take a local permit as well. For example, in the United States, you need a CITES permit as well as a permit from the Endangered Species Act. Check for regulations of the Wildlife department in your state, country and the country you are travelling to be safe.

The Blue and Gold Macaw is listed on the Appendix I of CITES. This means that your bird can be taken to another country only under certain circumstances. You will most likely need a permit form the country you are travelling and from the country you are travelling to.

Your veterinarian is a reliable source of information. He/she will be able to help you obtain these permits as well. You can check the official CITES website and the websites of the Wildlife departments of the countries involved.

Plan your travels well in advance because most permits take two months at least for processing. If you have to make a business trip urgently, you will most probably have to make alternate arrangements for your Macaw.

Here are a few things you need to have when you are planning a trip with your bird:

- Proof that your bird was legally obtained. A breeder's health certificate is usually accepted.
- The permit from the respective countries that you are going to travel to and from.
- Completed declaration forms as required in the destination port.
- A health certificate from your vet that is not more than 30 days old.

Take a few copies of your permits just to be sure. You also need to be prepared to be questioned by authorities at both ports to confirm the reason for the import or export of the bird. With all the documents in place, you will not have to worry about your bird too much. Just make sure that his wings are clipped to ease the process of customs.

Travelling with your bird by car

Getting your bird introduced to a car is a step-by-step process. It can demand a lot of patience from your end or it could be very easy to get your bird to love drives. It depends upon the personality of the bird and the measures you take to make this a positive experience for your bird.

- Step 1: Get the bird used to the car. Just transfer him to a smaller travelling cage and place the cage in the car. Make sure that the air conditioner is on. It is not advisable to leave windows open when you are travelling with birds as they may be stressed by drafts. If he shows discomfort take him home. Try this until the bird is used to the car and remains calm inside.

- Step 2: Take short drives around the block. Give the bird plenty of water and food to keep him calm. Of course, water should be given through a bottle to prevent any spilling on the way. Make sure that the cage is lined with lots of substrate. You can also give your bird a toy to stay calm. Then drive slowly and keep talking to the bird. He may be scared and may retreat to one corner of the cage. Keep the drive short and take him home. Do this until the bird is calm during these short trips.

- Step 3: Now your bird is ready for a long drive. Prepare the cage with food, water and substrate. If you have any bags to take with you, introduce these bags during the short rides so that the bird can get used to the colors and the shapes. Take breaks every half an hour to make sure that your bird is not stressed.

Travelling with your bird by air

If you have to travel overseas or move permanently, you will have to really think about it when you have a bird. If it is temporary, you may not want to stress the bird. It is best to leave your bird under someone else's care while you are away. However, if you have to move, you need to be sure that your bird is allowed in the state or country that you plan to move to. If he is not allowed there, you will have to either switch your moving plans or find him a foster home. The latter is very stressful for the bird. You see, having a Blue and Gold Macaw is like having a baby. Make him your top priority always. Unless you do not have any other options, it is not a kind thing to do to give your bird up. Before you travel overseas with your bird, here are a few things you need to do:

- Check with the Fish and Wildlife department of the place that you are traveling to about the restrictions with respect to Blue and Gold Macaws. In some countries and states, like Georgia, do not allow you

60

to have these birds as pets. Others require you to obtain a permit or a license to bring your bird to their country.

- You can contact your local Wildlife Department to check about the procedure to obtain a permit. Usually, you will be able to get a permit within 60 days of application to the concerned authority.

- Once the permit is in place, you need to find an airline that has the facilities to help you transport your bird safely. Read all the safety guidelines and provisions about livestock transport. Only when you are convinced should you opt for a certain airline. Make sure that all the transits are in the same airlines to prevent any sudden changes in the rules and regulations.

- Obtain a travelling cage as per the guidelines. Prepare the cage with water, food and substrate. In the case of long flights, the airline will provide feeding services for your bird. Keeping him harnessed is a good idea to keep him safe.

- Having the wings clipped is a great option, as it will prevent any drama during the customs and security checks. The bird is easier to handle and the chances of escaping are lower when his wings have been clipped.

- Upon reaching your destination, have your bird examined by the vet. He may have symptoms of stress such as vomiting and dizziness because of the flight and the change in altitude. Immediate examination will makes sure that he is safe.

- When you reach your new home, leave the bird in a quiet room with fresh water and food. Let him calm down and follow the same housebreaking procedure as mentioned above.

If you are unable to travel with your bird
In case you are unable to travel with your bird for legal or practical reasons, you need to ensure that you have your friends or family members on board to help. If that is not possible, you can also hire a professional pet sitter to take care of your bird for you.

Pet Sitters International is an organization that you can depend upon in order to find the best pet sitting services. They have a list of independent pet sitters or pet sitter agencies that you can contact.

It is recommended that you contact local bird clubs to find pet sitters who have worked for the members before and have taken good care of the birds. Friends and family with birds can also provide good recommendations for you.

Now, when you are looking for a pet sitter, you need to conduct an interview with a couple of them until you can find someone reliable enough to leave your bird with. During the interview sessions, there are a few pointers that you need to keep in mind to find the perfect caretaker for your bird.

- Ask for the pet sitters' experience. They should have some knowledge about handling birds and taking care of them. If you see that your pet sitter is a novice, you should know that he at least has birds of his own.

- Ask them what they know about Blue and Gold Macaws and if they have taken care of these birds in the past. The Blue and Gold Macaw is a large bird and has very specific requirements. One should know how to handle the bird at least.

- Ask if they have birds of their own. Anyone who has their own pets will also be sensitive to the requirements of other people. They will be sensitive and will understand that you need the best care for your bird. They are also aware of basic body language and will be able to communicate better with your bird. A pet sitter is not someone who will just feed the birds and clean the cage. They are literally taking your place while you are away.

- Observe the way he or she handles the bird. If they are comfortable with the bird and are able to manage him or her well, then they are probably quite experienced. They must also be able to calm a bird down when he is excited or aggressive.

- You need to make sure that he or she is capable of handling an emergency. Ask them how they would deal with various emergency situations. If it is close to what you would do, then you can hire this individual without a second thought.

- In your absence, if they have a personal emergency, how will they deal with it? Will they be able to send in a substitute? If yes, you need to meet the person who will be substituting for your pet sitter to ensure that they are right for your bird, too.

Once you have finalized a sitter, you need to discuss the cost and the services that he or she will provide. Make sure that you have it all in writing to prevent any confusion in the future.

Get all the contact details of your pet sitter including the phone number and email ID. You need to have access to him or her whenever you need. Make it a point to call every day to keep an eye on your bird.

Provide all the contact details of the place that you will be staying in. You also need to provide emergency contact numbers of friends and family members.

Make a written routine for your sitter to follow. You must even include the number of your vet in this list. Ensure that your pet sitter knows where the food is stocked, how to clean the food bowls and the cage and also where the first aid kit is located.

3. Teaching them to speak

This is an extremely fun activity to engage in with your bird. With a bird like the Blue and Gold Macaw, which is one of the most efficient in mimicking human voices and various types of sounds, you will find that this is one of the most fulfilling activities.

First, your Blue and Gold Macaw may pick up certain words on his own. If you say "Hello" or "Hi" every morning when you feed the bird, he will respond with the same words. If he hears a certain word or phrase over and over again, he is most likely to say it. So, watch what you say around your Blue and Gold Macaw. It is almost as good as having a child around who is learning to speak. You do not want him to learn any cuss words, so be very careful about what you say when the Blue and Gold Macaw is in the room. Sometimes, it could just be extremely embarrassing for you when he says something blasphemous in front of your guests.

Now, if you want to teach a Blue and Gold Macaw a specific word or phrase, you can do it by saying it over and over to him at a certain time of the day. Let us say you want to teach him to sing "Happy Birthday". You will have to find a time, maybe when you finish work or just before you leave for work. Sing one line of the song every day to him a couple of times. He will recite it back to you sooner or later. You can give a cue to him such as "Let's sing Happy Birthday" and then sing the song out. Sing one line at a time. When he picks up a full line, reward him and repeat it until he recites it easily. Then you can move on to the next few lines. Make sure you sing the lines he knows first and then the new lines so that he learns them in order.

You will see that the Blue and Gold Macaw spends a lot of time mumbling to himself. This is only him practicing the lines that he is learning. Other things that can help are playing the song you want him to learn on a DVD or on the TV. If you let your birds watch cartoons for 20 minutes a day, he is going to pick up a vast vocabulary before you know it.

Here are some songs that many Blue and Gold Macaw owners have taught their birds successfully:

- The nursery rhyme *Bingo*
- *You are my sunshine*
- *How much is that doggie in the window* By Pattie Page
- The nursery rhyme *I am a teapot.*

You can teach your Blue and Gold Macaw a host of different songs. Songs with repetitive and easy lyrics are the best ones for your bird.

4. Making your bird more social
When you are able to spend time with your bird and the people that you love, the bond strengthens even more. For this, your bird needs to be safe for people to interact with. You can socialize your Blue and Gold Macaw using some simple methods.

The first thing that you need to do is to train the macaw in basics like stepping up and even getting in and out of the cage. This is when your macaw is safe to introduce to your guests outside of a cage. Until you are sure that your macaw is through with this training, introducing them to strangers is not the best option.

Actually, as far as your Macaw is concerned, guests are invaders in their territory. In addition to this, when your guest is excited to see the gorgeous Blue and Gold Macaw and approaches the bird, it makes him feel helpless. There is another thing that a guest does - he takes the owner's attention away.

In short, having a guest is a negative experience for your bird. You need to make sure that you make it a fun thing for your macaw through positive reinforcements.

So, make sure that your Blue and Gold Macaw is well socialized, especially when it comes to meeting new people. Because these birds are so easy to train, you can follow these simple steps to make them friendly and also more approachable when you have guests at home.

- **Instruct your guest to ignore the bird:** If it is the first time someone is meeting your macaw, ask them to avoid even eye contact for the first 30-60 minutes. If your guest just goes for the cage, the bird will think that he means harm. However, let the guest stay in a room that the bird is able to watch over. That will let him understand that this person does not mean any harm and is actually welcome in the flock.

- **Let the bird out:** This should be done only if your bird is used to being handled. Let him out of the cage and let him be. The guest should be instructed not to approach the bird. Let the macaw take his time. These birds are extremely cautious, which means that sooner or later they will either walk over to the guest or will come to you to seek some security. This way, the bird does not get any reason to be scared and is more trusting towards new people.

- **Teach the guest to handle the bird:** Once the bird is comfortable to just hang around the new person, you can get them to handle it. Not everyone knows how to handle a pet bird, so you have to assist them. Even in the case of people who have had pet birds at home, you need to tell them how your bird likes to be handled. Macaws are different from pets like dogs and do not like to be heavily petted. It may turn them against the person, as they like to be treated with a lot of dignity.

- **Let them pretend to be a perch:** Extending the arm out and finger out and staying still is the best option. They should not reach out for the bird. Instead, you will let the bird go on to their arm or finger. Ask them not to move. Birds like macaws hate an unsteady perch. If your visitor is scared, do not force the bird upon them. If the person is scared, the bird will be scared and will certainly react.

Let the person cue tricks: If your macaw has been trained to perform tricks, then it is a wonderful icebreaker. When the bird is comfortable enough, let your guest cue the trick. Then, providing a treat for performing a trick gives the bird some reassurance. This is the safest and most fun way to get your bird to meet new people. It is a positive reinforcement plan that is sure to get your bird more interested in new people.

Tell the bird to step up: This can happen in the second meeting preferable or whenever the bird is fully comfortable with a person. Now, you will step out of the way and will not hand over the bird to the person. Instead, the guest will cue the step up command. Using a target or a treat the first time is a good idea. It is best to do this after the bird has been cued for other tricks. That makes him understand that the new person will give him treats if he does what he is asked to do. There is no room for doubt when the bird has already interacted to some extent.

- **Petting:** It is good to get your bird accustomed to being petted, but this should be reserved for when the bird is entirely confident about a certain person. You must guide the person and tell them exactly how your bird likes to be petted. For instance, they may love being scratched on the cheek and may hate being touched on the wing. If the person does the latter, be sure that your macaw will never let him or her touch him again. Start by petting the bird yourself first and let the guest join in. Then you can take your hand away and let the guest take over. This comfortable transition will make your bird look forward to new people being around.

- **Pass the bird around:** After your macaw is accustomed to a group of people, you can simply pass the bird around from one person to another at intervals. You can even add a resting perch in between, where the bird can relax while you entertain your guests. The basic idea is to make sure that your bird is used to many hands. This makes them trust people more and will also make them comfortable in front of a large crowd.

- **Make grabbing a positive thing:** Grabbing basically means holding the bird from the sides of the body. This training is essential, as it helps the bird stay relaxed when he is at the vet, when he is travelling by flights or even when he needs to be grabbed and taken out in an emergency. This is at a much later stage only with people whom the bird knows really well and trusts. They will begin by approaching the bird with a treat, holding on to him and then giving him a treat. This tells your bird that hands are not something that he needs to fear.

Your guest can begin by just touching the bird and giving him a treat, cupping the body and then giving him a treat and then proceeding to actually grabbing him. You will get them to repeat each step as many times as needed to make sure that your bird is completely comfortable before you actually get them to progress to getting their hands closer to the bird. Then, being handled becomes a regular activity for your bird and he will not feel scared.

- **Take the bird on outings:** Plan outdoor activities that involve your bird and a few other friends. It can begin with a family dinner or even a casual visit to a friend's place. This prevents the bird from being excessively territorial as he is on neutral grounds. That will make him less nippy and defensive and the interaction is more peaceful. Don't overwhelm the bird by taking him to a party or gathering with more than ten people.

- **Take the bird out:** Keeping the bird in the cage and going out for a stroll in the park has also helped many macaw owners claim that this helps the bird make observations and even be calmer in front of strangers, as they are accustomed to new faces. There may be people who will ask you if they can handle your bird. If you think that your bird is not aggressive, then you can instruct them to handle the bird safely. Only if they follow your instructions completely will you let them handle your bird.

- **Uncontrolled interactions:** Once your parrot is comfortable around people, let the interactions be less controlled. If there is a way you would recommend your bird be handled, let the person do just that. If the bird is harmless, he will only freak out momentarily and will get over it very soon. This makes them more robust and will not require you to intervene and protect him at all times.

No matter what you do, never predict how your bird is going to react in any situation. The last thing you want to take for granted in the temperament of your macaw. Remember that these birds are extremely intelligent and sensitive and will analyze each situation they are put in. Be around for all initial interactions and when you are certain that your bird is comfortable, let go slowly.

Chapter 5: Breeding Blue and Gold Macaws

Blue and Gold Macaws do not breed very readily, even in the wild. If you plan to breed your bird, then you need to make sure that you provide the specific conditions that the bird requires in order to mate.

Blue and Gold Macaws are ready to breed when they are about 3 years old. You can introduce a mate to your bird in the same way as you would introduce any bird to your pet. Follow the right quarantine methods and then assess the behavior of both birds before you allow them to breed.

Since Blue and Gold Macaws are not sexually dimorphic, surgical or DNA sexing is essential to know the gender of the birds.

Once you know that they are compatible, you can start the breeding process by taking the necessary measures.

1. Setting the nesting box

Once you have a compatible pair, you can set up a nesting box during the breeding season. It is a good idea to put this box outside the cage. If you have pets at home, you will have to put the birds away in a separate room that remains closed. The box is typically wide and deep. This gives the birds room to move around. A deep box means that the birds will not take the nesting material out. With Blue and Gold Macaws, they will exhibit nesting behavior and will try to hoard all thread like items in this box in an attempt to build a nest.

It is best to get a box that is made of wood. Wood helps the birds stay warm, as opposed to metal that can get cold. When the incubation period arrives, wood also retains moisture. The advantage with metal ones is that they last longer and are easier to clean. Make sure that the nesting box is secured tightly.

The opening for this box should be on top. If you provide a wooden nesting box, your Blue and Gold Macaws will chew them and modify them a little. Having a trap door at 1/3rd of the height of the box allows you to access the nesting box to feed the birds or remove the babies when the time comes. To help the birds climb in and out of the box, add a wire mesh strip from the top of the box to the bottom. This acts a ladder.

You can fill the nesting box almost all the way up to the opening with pine shavings. You can also use shredded newspaper. The birds will take out all the unwanted nesting material.

2. Diet

You need to give your bird a good diet to stay healthy during the breeding season. The female may require calcium supplements to ensure that the eggshells are intact. If your bird is still not on a full pellet diet, this is not the time to wean him. You should give the bird the regular diet to prevent any stress. You can just add vitamin and mineral supplements to their diet and even give them a cuttlebone to chew on.

Adding assorted nuts to the diet will help the bird to a large extent. Each nut has specific functions that aid the breeding season. Here are a few nuts that you should include and the benefits of these nuts:

- Macadamia nuts: They provide the additional fats that are required in a bird's diet during this season.
- Walnuts: They provide the birds with necessary omega 3 fatty acids.
- Filberts: They are a great source of calcium for the females.
- Pistachios: They aid vitamin A in large amounts.
- If your bird is already on a pellet diet with fresh produce, you only have to worry about giving them the pellets recommended for the breeding period. No added supplementation is necessary with pellets, as they are already fortified. You can place a cuttlebone just in case and the bird will chew on it if she needs the calcium.

3. Egg laying

After about 25 hours of the fertilization of the egg, the female will lay the first egg. She will lay about 2-3 eggs, laying one each day. She will have a second clutch of eggs after a month. If you want the bird not to lay the second clutch, you can reduce daytime to about 10 hours. You can move the birds to a dark room or could just turn the light off early. Just when the bird is about to lay the first egg, her droppings become smelly and large. She will also show evident abdominal distension.

If you see that the hen is leaving the eggs dormant without sitting on them, you will have to increase the temperature of the nest using an aquarium heater. Parrots are known for abandoning their clutch. If you see that your bird does not sit on the eggs and incubate them even after increasing the temperature, you will have to incubate the eggs artificially.

If the hen does brood, the incubation period is about 28 days.

4. Artificial Incubation

To incubate the eggs, you can purchase a standard incubator from any pet supplies store. You can also order them online. It is never advisable to prepare your own incubator, as the temperature settings need to be very accurate to hatch the eggs successfully. The incubation period will be the same as the natural incubation period.

The incubator is a one-time investment that is completely worth it if you choose to breed more Blue and Gold Macaws even in the next season.

Here are a few tips to incubate the eggs correctly:

- Pick the eggs up with clean hands. The chicks are extremely vulnerable to diseases and can be affected even with the smallest traces of microbes. Only pick eggs that are visibly clean. If there is a lot of debris or poop on a certain egg, it is best not to mix it with the other eggs, as it will cause unwanted infections.

- Wash the eggs gently to clean the surface. The next step is to candle the eggs. This means you will have to hold the egg up to a light. If you can see the embryo in the form of a dark patch, it means that the egg is fertile. On the other hand, if all you can see is an empty space inside the egg, it is probably not going to hatch.

- In the natural setting, the eggs are usually given heat on one side while the other side remains cooler. Then the bird may turn the eggs with her movements. It is impossible to heat the egg evenly even if you have a fan type incubator that heats up the interior of the egg quite evenly.

- The next thing to keep in mind is the transfer from the nest box to the incubator. Line a container with wood shavings and place the eggs away from each other. Even the slightest bump can crack an egg. You need to know that a cracked egg has very few chances of hatching.

- The incubator will also have a humidifier that will maintain the moisture levels inside the incubator. The temperature and the humidity should be set as per the readings advised for macaws. That is the ideal condition for the eggs to hatch.

- If you want to be doubly sure, you can also check the temperature with a mercury thermometer regularly.

- It is safest to place the eggs on the side when you put them in the incubator. They are stable and will not have any damage or accident.

- Heating the eggs evenly is the most important thing when it comes to the chances of hatching the egg. Make sure you turn the eggs every two hours over 16 hours. This should be done an odd number of times. The next step is to turn the eggs by 180 degrees once every day.

- Keep a close watch on the eggs in the incubator. It is best that you get an incubator with a see-through lid. This will let you observe and monitor the eggs. If you notice that one of them has cracked way before the incubation period ends, take it out of the incubator. If the eggs have a foul smelling discharge, begin to take an abnormal shape or change color, you need to remove them as they could be carrying diseases that will destroy the whole clutch.

- Usually, Blue and Gold Macaw eggs will pip after 24-48 hours of the completion of the incubation period.

- The hatching of the egg begins when the carbon dioxide levels in the egg increase. This starts the hatching process. All baby birds have an egg tooth, which allows them to tear the inner membrane open. Then they continue to tear the eggshell to come out.

- The muscles of the chick twitch in order to strengthen them and to make sure that he is able to tear the eggshell out successfully.

- Never try to assist the hatching process unless you are a professional. If you feel like your chicks are unable to break out of the eggshell, you can call your vet immediately.

Watching the eggs hatch is a magical experience. You can do a few small things to make your clutch more successful. For instance, if you are buying a brand new incubator, turn on the recommended settings and keep it on for at least two weeks before you expect the eggs to be placed in them.

Make sure that the incubator is not disturbed. Keep all the wires tucked in to prevent someone from tripping on it and disturbing the set up or turning the incubator off. It is best to place this incubator in areas like the basement that are seldom used by you or your family members.

5. Raising the chicks

Towards the end of the incubation period, you need to set up a brooding box, which can either be purchased or even created using a simple cardboard box. This is where the chicks will be raised until they are large enough to feed on their own and occupy a cage.

Now, this box needs to have an internal temperature of 36 degrees centigrade. You can maintain this using a heating lamp. If you do not feel confident to do this, you can just buy a readymade brooder. These brooders have recommended settings that will ensure that your bird is in safe hands.

As soon as the egg hatches, the hatchlings should be shifted to this brooder or brooding box.

Young birds are seldom able to feed on their own. You will have to make sure that you give the birds the nutrition that they need by hand-feeding them.

Your vet will be able to recommend a good baby bird formula that you can feed the hatchlings. All you have to do is mix the formula as per the instructions on the box. Then using a clean syringe or ink dropper, you can feed the babies.

When you are feeding the bird, make sure that you place him on a towel because this is going to be a rather messy task. Then hold the head of the bird between two fingers and push the upper jaw gently. The bird will open his mouth automatically. Then, you will have to hold the syringe to the left of the bird's mouth or to your right and then let the food in. This ensures that your bird does not choke on the food that you are giving him.

When the birds are done eating, they will automatically refuse the feed. You will have to feed hatchlings at least once every two hours. Make sure that you watch the body language of the bird. If he is resisting the feed, you can wait a little longer and then do the same.

As the birds grow, the number of feeding sessions will reduce. Ideally, by the time the feathers of the birds appear, they will be feeding about three times every day.

The next step is to wean the birds or make them independent eaters. This can be done when the birds are about 7 weeks old. You can introduce solid foods like pellets and fruits to the bird along with the handfed formula.

Just place a few pieces of fruit or some pellets in front of the bird and wait for him to taste it. If he likes it, he may eat a little and then move on to the formula. Try introducing different fruits and vegetables and notice which ones are tempting enough for the bird to leave the formula for.

You can replace one meal with the favorite food of the bird and add a few pellets too. You will notice that eventually the birds will eat when they are hungry and will not accept the hand fed formula. That is when they are fully weaned.

Incubating the egg artificially has several advantages. To begin with, it encourages the parent birds to lay another clutch of eggs. Next, it increases the chances of the egg hatching. As for hand feeding, it makes your birds familiar with people and will also make them easier to train. Blue and Gold Macaws are known to be bad at parenting and are notorious for leaving their babies hungry.

On the other hand, when a bird is raised by the parents, they will develop a parenting instinct that is better than that of a hand fed bird. They are likely to be better breeders.

The best thing to do would be to allow the birds to feed the little ones for a while. Then you can intervene and help the babies wean. This is called mixed parenting and is best for those who intend to breed Blue and Gold Macaws commercially.

6. Weaning the chicks

You know that the bird is ready to be weaned when he starts handling small objects with his beak or tries to climb using the beak. You will now reduce the formula to twice a day and introduce the bird to eating on his own. Weaning basically means that you are getting the bird to a stage when he can eat on his own without your help or the parent's help.

Place the babies in a cage that is lined with newspaper. Place a feeding bowl and a water bowl in it. You need one for each chick and it should be shallow enough for the bird to eat from. It is recommended that you put the bird into this cage after hand feeding in the morning. If the birds are very hungry, they may refuse to eat on their own.

You will be able to attract the babies to the new food, preferably special baby pellets, by mixing in rice crispies. You will see that they do not mind experimenting as long as their tummy isn't fully empty. Eventually they will stop eating in the evening. Then they will slowly take to eating on their own and will wean with time. Never rush the baby. Prepare a feeding routine and stick to it and they will eventually learn to eat all their food on their own.

7. How to hand feed the baby birds

You will have two options to choose from once the babies have hatched. You may allow the parents to feed and raise the babies in which case the birds are more social towards other birds. The other option is to hand feed the bird and make the tame. It really depends upon what you plan to do with the hatchlings.

If you decide to hand feed the birds, the ideal age to remove them from the cage is when they are about 3-4 weeks old. This is when the birds are in their pinfeather stage. Their feathers look like quills at this stage. This is the best age, as the birds are able to hold the body heat and will not require any artificial heat. These birds also have the advantage of being raised by their parents and will be healthier. Immunity is better as the parents will pass on antibodies while feeding the babies.

Choose a formula recommended by your vet. Prepare the formula as per the instructions on the package. You need to make sure that the formula is heated to about 100 degrees F and not more than that. This can scald the insides of the delicate baby bird.

It is better to use a spoon to feed the baby as opposed to a syringe as you will be able to control the food going into the belly of the baby. That way you reduce the risk of choking the baby. Feeding with a spoon is much slower, so the chances of overfeeding are fewer. When the baby is full, you will be able to see the signs that will tell you when to stop feeding. You will also spend more time with the baby when you feed him with a spoon.

In case you pull the babies out of the nest earlier or have to hand feed them at an earlier stage because they were artificially incubated, you will have to purchase a brooder that will keep the babies warm as you feed them. The formula must be made very watery and should be given to the bird in small quantities. Then you wait for the crop to empty and feed the baby again. At a very young age, you may have to feed the baby every two hours.

In the pinfeather stage, you can feed the baby 4-5 times and give him some time to rest overnight. That way the crop will be fully empty and he will be ready for next meal.

Chapter 6: Health of Blue and Gold Macaws

Blue and Gold Macaws require the right surroundings in order to be healthy. Making sure that you have the right avian vet is the first step to keeping your bird safe and healthy. Regular medical examinations along with the right precautionary measures are the key to ensuring that your bird is free from any diseases.

Like most parrots, Blue and Gold Macaws are also great at hiding any illnesses. This is a natural instinct, as the birds do not want to seem vulnerable to predators in the wild. Keeping a close eye on your bird is necessary to detect any health issues early and have it treated to prevent any fatalities.

1. The right vet for your bird

Healthcare is the most important thing for your bird. If you do not have the assistance of a good avian vet, you will find it challenging to ensure that your bird gets the best medical aid possible. Annual checkups with an avian vet can be life saving for your bird in many cases.

Vets that treat regular pets like cats and dogs will not be able to help your bird with specific illnesses like PDD or PBFD, which we will discuss in the following chapters.

You will have to look for an avian vet who specializes in treating exotic birds.

The first step is to locate an avian vet near you. You can look up the website of the Association of Avian Vets to search for certified vets location-wise. If that does not help you find a vet close to your home, you can even enquire at the office of vets who treat other pets or in the pet supply store. Your breeder will be able to help you the best.

Avian vets hold a degree in veterinary studies just like the other vets. However, they specialize in treating birds and a major part of their practice consists of working with birds and diseases related to exotic birds.

In the case of the Blue and Gold Macaw, it is a good idea to look for an Avian vet who is a member of the Association of Avian Vets.

What is the Association of Avian Vets?

This organization was founded in the year 1980 with the intention of improving the practices of Avian medicine. The members of this group comprise mostly of private veterinarians, veterinarians working for zoos, students of veterinary sciences as well as technicians in the field of avian medicine.

The advantage with a vet who is a part of this organization is that he or she will be up to date with all the latest trends and practices in the field of avian medicine. Through regular conferences and online educational material, the AAV reaches out to all its members with the necessary information to upgrade their practice.

The goal of the AAV is to make sure that the veterinarians associated with it become more competent. If you have found a vet who is a member of the AAV, credibility is something that you do not have to worry about.

With the AAV, the idea of promoting these birds as companions and valuable possessions is of utmost importance. This ensures that the vets associated with this organization will be sensitive towards your beloved pet and will make sure that they get the best services available.

Even for bird owners, the AAV works hard to help them understand how important veterinary care is for the well being of their bird. They are encouraged to look for only qualified vets. With the massive backing of this organization, the good news is that the number of these vets is fast growing. Therefore, it is easier to find qualified avian vets who can take good care of exotic birds these days.

Learn more about your avian vet

When you have finally located a good avian vet, the next step is to make sure that they are the right people to entrust your bird with. Even if a vet is not associated with the AAV, the confidence with which he or she answers the following questions will help you decide if you want to be associated with them in the long run or not.

- **How many years have you been treating birds for?** As you know, expertise comes with experience. If your vet has a good background with treating birds, you can be certain that your birds are in safe hands.

- **Are you familiar with Blue and Gold Macaws?** New world parrots can be very different from Old world parrots. Of course, parrots have a totally different response to certain treatments in comparison to other birds. So, if you are looking for a vet for your Blue and Gold Macaw, the best thing to do would be to look for someone with enough experience with this species.

- **Do you have your own pet birds?** Anyone who has their own pet will be sensitive to the bond that you share with your bird and will be available for most emergencies without any complaints. These people are also likely to understand the body language of your bird and will be able to pick up on even the most subtle signs of illnesses that can help in diagnosing the health issue.

- **Are emergency services available?** If your vet has a pet hospital with an emergency room, it is the best option for you. You must also ask for afterhours help in case your bird has any emergency. If your vet is not able to provide this service, he or she will be able to suggest other facilities that can be of great help to you.

- **Will you make house calls?** Sometimes the bird may be too sick to travel with you to the vet. In case of accidents resulting in skull or leg fractures, you must not even move the bird to keep the condition from getting worse. Your vet should be willing to make house calls or must be able to send one a staff member at the very least.

- **How many checkups will be required in a year?** A good vet will suggest that you get at least one checkup each year to ensure that your bird is in good health. Anyone who is not too concerned about the annual checkup is not genuinely interested in the well being of your bird.

The tone of your vet and the confidence with which he or she answers these questions will help you understand how genuine they are in their interests to treat your bird. If they seem too standoffish and unpleasant, you can always move on to other vets who will be happy to have you.

While you are at it, observe the way the vet interacts with your birds and other patients. A warm and welcoming vet will be able to make this experience less stressful for the birds. He or she should be confident in holding and handling the bird. If the examinations take place with the birds in the cage in all cases, you are possibly not in the right hands.

Every examination must be thorough and complete. If your vet is seeing one patient every 15 minutes then you can be sure that this is an extremely commercial practice that will not pay close attention to your beloved pet.

Some of these avian vets may treat other pets as well. However, the frequency of the number of feathered patients should be high. If an individual claims to be an avian vet but you only see one bird or two of them over the day, he/she is probably not best suited for your Blue and Gold Macaw.

The staff will also say a lot about the facility. They should be familiar with your bird's type. If they are well-trained professionals, they will also not have any trouble handling the bird. Watch the way they interact with other pets and pet parents. Are they cheerful? Or are they just interested in getting them in line for the appointments?

Take a good look around the facility. Is it well maintained and sterilized? If they have in patient services, do each of the birds have their own housing areas. If yes, how are these housing areas maintained? Remember, the pet hospital can be a big source of germs and microbes that will infect your bird. They should also have facilities like gram scales, updated instruments and well maintained equipment.

When you are convinced about the person that you have approached, you can assign them with the role of being the caretaker of your bird's health.

While you are at it, you can even ask about the insurance policies available for pet birds. Some of them will cover most medical expenses in case of an emergency and will also be able to provide third party liability in case of any damage caused by your bird to another person's property. Your vet will be associated with certain health insurance companies that can help you take care of all the medical expenses with respect to your bird.

Usually, these insurance policies have a premium of $100-250 or £50 to 100 depending on the cover that you are looking at. However, they are worth the investment as you will be able to get a lot of support when your bird requires any emergency care or assistance. Last minute expenses can be very stressful if your bird does not have insurance.

In addition to that, insurance will come in very handy when you are travelling with your bird. Most airlines insist that your bird be insured before taking them on board. For the medical expenses, you also have the option of opening a savings account that you can set aside some money in on a monthly basis to help in case of an emergency.

2. What preventive measures should you take?
There is no better way to keep your bird healthy than preventive care. Since most illnesses spread so fast in Blue and Gold Macaws, it is best that you take all the precautionary steps possible to prevent this sort of

infection in the first place. Here are some tips that will help you maintain the health of your little feathered companion:

- Make sure that the diet is wholesome and nutritious

- Clean the cage and its contents regularly

- Take your pet to the vet for an annual checkup without fail

- Any new bird that is introduced to your home must be quarantined without fail

- The bird must have a lot of clean water to drink

- Your bird must be mentally stimulated in order to ensure good health

- Spend enough time with your bird to prevent any behavioral problems

- You need to make sure that he gets ample sunlight. It is a good idea to take the bird outdoors provided he is harnessed or is protected by a cage

- Your home must be bird proofed even before you bring the bird home

- Grooming and cleaning the bird is necessary.

Always keep your vet's number handy and learn as much as you can about your Blue and Gold Macaw's health. That way, communicating with the vet also becomes easier and you will be able to provide better care for your bird.

3. Idenitifying health issues in your bird

Many parrot owners have spoken about unexpected deaths of their pets. While there are some diseases that have very low incubation periods, most can be detected quite easily at an early stage if the owner is able to recognize the signs of illness in the bird. This is what you need to watch out for:

- Abnormal droppings: The droppings of the bird are the first sign of any illness. The consistency of the poop and its color determine which part of the body has been affected. These are a few abnormalities that you need to keep in mind:
    - Any air pockets in the poop is a sign of gas development in the bird's gut.

-        Droppings which are black or red in color is a sign of egg binding, infection of the intestine or internal bleeding that may be caused by swallowing a foreign object.

-        If any undigested food is excreted, it shows that the bird may have problems in the pancreas or has an infection of some sort.

-        Diarrhea or loose stools is a sign of multiple issues like infections, parasites or even digestive issues.

-        If your bird has been dropping very liquidy poop for more than two days, it is a sign of some infection in the kidney.

-        If the urine content or the transparent liquid part of the poop is low, your bird is possibly dehydrated.

-        If the semi solid part of the dropping is yellow or green in color, it suggests a liver condition.

-        If the urine is yellow in color, it is a chance of a kidney condition.

•   There are fluctuations in the weight: You need to have a gram scale in your home and measure your bird from time to time. Of course, there are minute changes based on how much your bird has eaten, the pooping cycle, etc. However, if you notice that your bird has lost more than 10% of his total body weight, you need to consult your vet immediately.

•   Change in physical appearance: You will notice signs like discoloration of feathers, puffed up feathers and dried poop near the vent. There could be other signs that raise caution. Remember that Blue and Gold Macaws are fastidious in keeping their body clean. So, a bird who looks messy is possibly unwell.

•   Loss of appetite: Blue and Gold Macaws are good eaters. However, if you notice that they are leaving their food untouched, it is a matter of concern. Even if your bird does not seem fatigued or low in energy, a loss of appetite is a sign of possible illness.

•   Withdrawn body language: If your bird retreats to one corner of the cage and spends most of the time on the floor, he is showing signs of illness. In addition to that, the feathers may droop and he may even keep his beak hidden under the wings.

• Discharge of fluids: If you see any discharge from the nasal passage or the eyes, it is a sign of infection. This needs to be attended to immediately.

• Inactivity: Blue and Gold Macaws are extremely active birds. They love to climb, fly and play. If your bird is less vocal or shows a sudden drop in his levels of physical activity, rush him to a vet immediately.

• Cloudy eyes: A Blue and Gold Macaw has beady eyes that always sparkle like they are up to some mischief. But, when they are unwell, the eyes become dull and seem quite cloudy.

These are the most common signs of illness in Blue and Gold Macaws. Of course, they may develop other behavioral problems like biting or fear of people when they are hurt or unwell. Even if it is no illness at all, when you notice the slightest deviation from normal, take your bird to a vet immediately. As they say, prevention is better than cure, especially in birds that can develop fatal conditions overnight.

4. Common macaw diseases

There are a few infections and diseases that you need to know about as they commonly affect the Blue and Gold Macaw as a species. We will talk about the identification, the cause and the cure for these conditions in the following section:

Proventricular Dilation Disease

This condition is also known as Macaw Wasting Syndrome. In the past, this condition was considered to be fatal most of the time. However, new treatment methods have emerged over the years, which makes it possible to control the symptoms in the early stages.

This condition is caused by the Avian Bornavirus, which is believed to have spread rampantly due to pet trade across the world. These viruses invade the cell of the host and continue to infect more cells eventually. The incubation period for this virus is about 4 weeks. It affects younger birds usually although a Blue and Gold Macaw is vulnerable at any age, especially during the breeding season. It can be spread from the hen to the eggs as well.

The common signs of PDD are:

- Poor digestion
- Traces of undigested foods in the feces
- Sudden increase or decrease in appetite
- Weight loss
- Depression
- Anorexia
- Lack of coordination
- Seizures
- Muscle deficiencies
- Feather plucking
- Constant crying or moaning.

The treatment of this condition includes the administration of anti-inflammatory drugs that can soothe the symptoms. However, the infection itself is seldom cured. Supplements like milk thistle and elemental formula for birds are also recommended.

Psittacine Beak and Feather Disease

With this condition, the cells of the feather and beak are killed by a strain of virus called the circovirus. This disease also impairs the immune system of the bird, leading to death of the bird from other infections in most cases.

This condition was first noticed among cockatoos but has affected several species of birds, mostly those belonging to the Psittacine family.

In most cases, death follows the infection. However, if the bird responds positively to the tests but has no signs of the diseases physically, it means that he or she is a carrier of the condition. This is when you have to quarantine the bird immediately. This is a contagious disease that spreads very easily.

The common signs of PBFD are:

- Abnormalities in the feathers
- Bumps and uneven edges in the beak
- Missing lumps of feathers
- Loss of appetite
- Diarrhea
- Regurgitation

In most cases, the birds will die before they show the above symptoms.

Treatment of the condition includes administering probiotics and mineral or vitamin supplementation. The only way to curb PBFD is to take preventive measures such as maintaining good sanitation and diet.

Psittacosis

This condition is also known as Chlamydiosis or Parrot fever. The threat with this condition is that it can also affect human beings. It is a condition caused by a certain strain of bacteria called the Chlamydia Psittaci.

A few species of birds may never show symptoms of this condition and could be mere carriers. However, the fact that humans are susceptible to the condition requires you to take additional precautions.

This bacterial infection is only spread when you come into contact with the feces of the bird. This is true for other birds as well. So, maintaining good hygiene is the first step towards preventing this condition among the other birds in your aviary. You must also make sure that your birds are not exposed to the feces of wild birds when you let them out. The common problems leading to chlamydiosis are overcrowding of the aviary, improper quarantine measures, etc.

The common signs of Chlamydiosis or Psittacosis are:
- Labored breathing
- Infection of the sinuses
- Runny nasal passage
- Discharge and swelling of the eyes
- Ruffled feathers
- Lethargy
- Dehydration
- Weight loss
- Abnormal droppings.

These are the mild symptoms of the condition. In the case of a chronic case of Psittacosis you will observe unusual positioning of the head, tremors, lack of co-ordination, paralysis of the legs and loss of control over the muscles.

The birds suspected with this condition are tested for a high WBC count and an increase in liver enzymes, which suggests liver damage. Antibiotics like Doxycycline and Tetracycline are usually administered to affected birds. In addition to that, supplements and medicated foods are also provided. However, because most birds refuse to eat when affected with this condition, it becomes a lot harder to give them proper treatment.

Aspergillosis

This is a condition that is non contagious but highly infectious. The fungus that causes this condition is known as AspergillusFumigatus and is known to be very opportunistic. That is why even the slightest signs of dampness will become breeding grounds for this fungi.

Young birds are mostly susceptible to this condition. In the case of juvenile or baby birds, the rate of mortality is extremely high. Of course, in the case of adult birds, they could become infected too. The spores of this fungus are easily inhaled, as they are extremely small. That is why the infection is mostly seen in the air capillaries of the affected bird.

The most common signs of aspergillosis include:

- Polydipsia or abnormal thirst
- Stunted growth
- Lethargy
- Ruffled feathers
- Anorexia
- Polyuria or large amounts of urine in the excreta
- Wheezing
- Coughing
- Nasal Discharge
- Tremors
- Ataxia or loss of control over the limbs
- Cloudy eyes.

This condition mainly affects the respiratory tract. However, other organs may also be affected in some rare cases of infection. Treatment of this condition is challenging because of the loss of immunity in birds, so the affected bird could also have multiple infections caused by other microorganisms. Normally, systemic antifungal therapy is recommended. The lesions caused at the site of infection may also be removed through suction or surgery.

Preventive care is the best way to keep your bird safe. Maintaining a high standard of husbandry will help you control infections by depriving the fungus of any breeding sites.

Avian sinusitis

It is quite common for the sinuses of the birds to get infected. This condition is mostly associated with a deficiency in Vitamin A. This leads to abnormal cell division that will be seen in the form of thickened mucus around the eyes. This can further lead to abscesses or conjunctivitis if the affected bird. There are debates about the causal factor, however.

The earliest signs of this condition are:
- Clicking
- Proptosis or protrusion of the eyeball
- Sneezing
- Excessive secretion of mucus.

Later on, you will notice that there is swelling around the eyes as well as the region around the beak of the bird. When the sinus is infected, it is also possible for the bird to be suffering from associated conditions such as pneumonia.

A needle biopsy of the area with swelling helps diagnose the condition. This helps you differentiate the condition from abscesses that require a completely different treatment altogether.

The bird is treated with an antibiotic called Baytril that can curb any infection by bacteria such as pseudomonas. In addition to this, the bird also requires Vitamin A supplementation, which may be administered through an intramuscular injection. The sinus is flushed if the swelling is too much.

You must also improve the diet of the bird and include as many dark green vegetables as possible. Oranges are also recommended to improve the condition. Lastly, you need to include only fortified pellets in your bird's diet to help restore the Vitamin A levels in the body.

Psittacine Herpes Virus

Also known as Pacheco's disease, this condition was first recognized in the country of Brazil. Aviculturists observed that birds began to die within few days of being unwell. In less than 3-4 days, a herpes virus infection will cause nasal discharge and abnormal feces. This condition is very contagious and is often fatal.

New World parrots like the Blue and Gold Macaw are more susceptible to this condition. This condition is generally transmitted through the feces or the nasal discharge. The problem with this virus is that it remains stable even outside the body of the host.

It will be seen on different surfaces in the cage, the food and the water bowls. As a result, it spreads quite easily. Of course, there are possibilities of transmission of this condition from the mother to the embryo.

In many cases, a bird could be a mere carrier of the condition without any symptoms. A bird that has survived an infection is a potential threat to you flock.

The symptoms of this condition commonly include:
- Ruffled feathers
- Diarrhea
- Sinusitis
- Anorexia
- Conjunctivitis
- Tremors in the neck, legs and wings
- Lethargy
- Weight loss
- Green colored feces.

In most cases, death occurs due to enlargement in the liver or the spleen. When subjected to stress and sudden climate changes, the virus can get activated in birds that are carriers, leading to their death.

A PCR test is conducted to screen the birds for a herpes virus infection. In some cases a bird that is tested positive could show no symptoms at all.

There is no known cure for this condition. Only preventive measures can be taken by keeping the cage conditions pristine. You also need to ensure that your bird does not undergo any stress or trauma. When he is not well exercised or mentally stimulated, there are chances of activation of this strain of virus.

Coacalpapillomas

This is yet another condition that is said to be caused by a strain of virus called Papillomavirus. This condition leads to benign tumors in the regions of the bird's body that are un-feathered. There are a few debates about the causal factors of this condition, however. This is because of the internal lesions detected with this condition that is caused by a strain of Herpes virus.

Common symptoms of the condition include:
- Wart-like growths on the legs and feet
- Loose droppings
- Dried fecal matter around the vent area
- Blood in the droppings of the bird.

In case you suspect this condition in your macaw, you can make a preemptive diagnosis at home. Apply a small amount of 5% acetic acid on the cloacal region. If this turns white, then your bird is most likely infected.

Proper diagnosis includes a biopsy of the tissue that is affected. The growth on the legs and feet will be removed surgically as the first step to treatment. This condition leads to a compromised immune system that can further lead to secondary infections by bacteria and other microorganisms.

If your bird harbors any internal papillomas, you need to have them monitored frequently for any infection in the GI tract. If left ignored, it can lead to tumors in the bile duct or the pancreas.

Kidney dysfunction

There are two kinds of kidney dysfunction that you will observe in bird:

Chronic renal failure: This is when the kidney becomes progressively dysfunctional. At the onset, the bird will show very few signs and will only seem mildly under the weather.

Acute renal failure: This is when both the kidneys fail and deteriorate rapidly. The condition is usually reversible but the kidneys will be compromised to a great extent.

So, how can you tell if your bird has any developed of these kidney diseases:
- Polydipsia or excessive water consumption followed by frequent urination is common. This is the bird's attempt to flush out toxins from the blood, as the kidney is unable to perform this function effectively.
- Watery droppings
- Enlargement of the abdomen
- Constipation
- Vomiting
- Inability to fly
- Fluffing of feathers

- Depression
- Lethargy
- Weakness
- Blood in the droppings
- Dehydration
- Swollen joints
- Inability to walk or balance.

These renal diseases can be caused by microbial infections. The common virus responsible for this condition is the Polyomavirus while the most common fungus seen is the Aspergillus fungi.

There are various other causes like excessive vitamin D consumption, allergy to any antibiotics or medication that has been administered, heavy metal poisoning, toxicity by pesticides and ingestion of certain plants.

Gout, which is the inability of the bird to release waste from the body, also leads to kidney failure over time.

Proper diagnosis of this condition requires a full medical history of the bird. This is followed by a physical examination, blood chemistry tests, blood count tests and a urine analysis. In ambiguous cases, cloacal swabs, endoscopy and ultrasound are used to confirm the condition that the bird has been affected with.

Supportive care including tube feeding and providing the right supplements aids the recovery of the bird. It is recommended that the blood of the bird be tested on a regular basis to change the treatment method as required by the body of the bird.

Antibiotics may be administered as bacteria is the common cause of renal failure in birds. There could also be some secondary infections that need to be treated with antibiotics. Besides this, depending upon the nature of the infection, antifungal and antiviral medicines are provided.

In case of toxicity or gout, vitamin A supplementation is encouraged. There could also be surgical intervention if tumors or lesions are detected internally.

It is recommended that you include proteins, vitamin B complex, Vitamin C and Vitamin A in the diet of the bird. Foods like dandelion root, Cranberry, Parsley and Nettle tea will help improve the functioning of the kidneys and will aid in quick recovery of the affected bird.

Lymphomas or Tumors

It is possible for pet birds to develop tumors or lymphomas on their bodies. These are usually seen as bumps or lumps on the skin or just under the skin. Of course, every lump is not an indication of a tumor, as some of them could also be abscesses.

In many cases, what is feared to be a tumor could be a cyst that is covered with fluids or pus. These are not cancerous and will not spread like the tumors.

A tumor is a solid tissue mass that can grow very quickly and spread across the body of the bird. It can occur in any part of the body and needs immediate attention to ensure that your bird is able to recover from it.

There are two kinds of tumors: Benign and malignant. The benign tumors do not cause cancer while the malignant ones are cancerous. While both can adversely affect the health of the bird, benign tumors are less urgent that malignant ones.

The reason for this is that the benign tumors do not spread to other parts of the bird's body like the malignant ones. There are chances of growth in this tumor but they almost never spread. Even if they do, there is enough time to provide medical care effectively.

That does not mean that you can ignore these tumors. They need to be removed at the earliest. Since they get bigger in size, they can put a lot of pressure on the internal organs of the bird, leading to severe discomfort and even damage.

Malignant tumors will damage the nearby tissues of the affected organ as well. A process called metastasis is responsible for this. This is when the cell breaks away from the tumor and travels through the blood stream. Then it spreads to various parts of the body to cause multiple tumors.

Usually a tumor is caused by mutations in the DNA of the bird's cells. Normal cells will not divide uncontrollably like the tumors. They multiply enough to grow and repair the body.

There are several other factors like the environment of the bird, the inclusion of carcinogens in the diet of the bird, nutritional deficiencies, old age and interbreeding that compromise the immune system of the bird, leading to this condition.

There are various types of tumors that can affect a bird. The most common one is that of the skin or the squamous cells of the skin. This leads to tumors near the eyes, around the preen gland, and on the skin on the head and around the beak. A huge causal factor for this is self-mutilation by the birds. This is an external tumor that you can identify as lumps on the surface of the skin.

Another type of tumor that affects birds is a fibroid tumor. This affects the connective tissues of the bird. Usually, these tumors are benign. When they become malignant, the condition is known as fibrosarcoma. These tumors are also external and will be seen on the legs, wings, the beak and the sternum of the bird.

The most common type of internal tumor is a tumor in the reproductive organs or the kidneys. Again, these tumors could either be malignant or benign. The problem with these internal tumors is that they will go unnoticed until the bird falls severely sick. The pressure of these tumors on the internal organs leads to a lot of discomfort and stress for the birds. In most cases, the digestive system experiences a lot of stress, leading to improper digestion of food. The droppings are not excreted effectively from the body either. It can also put a lot of pressure on the nervous system, making the bird uncoordinated.

Birds can also develop cancers in the lymphatic system. This compromises the immune system to a large extent leading to secondary bacterial, viral or fungal infections. When the tumor is malignant, the condition is known as lymphoma. It is characterized by swollen lymph nodes in most cases.

Another type of tumor in the birds are lipomas. These are made mostly of mature fat cells. You will find these tumors just under the skin of the bird near the abdomen and he chest. They interfere with the body movements and will also lead to lethargy and inactivity. These are normally seen in obese birds.

Tumors that are external are easily identified as they appear in the form of lumps. Any abnormal growth on the body should be shown to the vet immediately. A pathologist will examine samples from the affected area and will determine if it is a tumor or not. The next step is to check if it is malignant or benign.

The internal tumors are really hard to detect. You will notice symptoms like:

- Weight loss
- Increased sleep
- Loss of appetite
- Inability to balance the body
- Lameness.

These symptoms could be indicative of any other disease as well, so you need to have your bird checked by a vet the moment you notice them.

The treatment of tumors or lipomas includes surgical removal of the mass of cells. If the tumor is growing or changing and is located in a part of the body that can affect its daily activities, surgery is avoided.

The prognosis of benign tumors is definitely better than the malignant ones. It could just require removal of the tissue in most cases.

It is the malignant tumors that are harder to treat. This is because they may continue to spread even after removal, unless they are removed at a very early stage.

Tumors of the kidney, the liver and other vital organs are the hardest to deal with as they could lead to death of the bird during surgery due to excessive bleeding.

In the case of Blue and Gold Macaws, it is a lot easier thanks to the size of the birds. The larger the animal, the easier it is to carry out surgical processes.

In rare cases, radiation and chemotherapy may help control these malignant tumors. They will be used in conjunction with surgical processes.

This is a very recent practice in avian medicine. That is why most avian vets will have less experience with providing radiation to birds. However, when there are very few avenues of treatment, radiation may be used on an experimental basis.

The drugs used in chemotherapy are very harsh. Since birds are easily susceptible to toxicity, there are chances that the bird dies of poisoning in the course of this treatment.

If the tumor is malignant, there is very little chance of survival unless the bird is treated in the initial stages. That is why it is recommended to take your bird for regular check-ups by the veterinarian. That way the tests will be able to detect internal tumors, if any.

Toxicity

Heavy metal poisoning due to metals like zinc and lead is quite common in pet birds. This is because of the several sources of toxicity that we neglect while getting the house bird proofed.

Zinc poisoning:

The discomfort caused depends on the amount of toxins that are present in the body of the bird. There are some signs of toxicity that you need to watch out for:
- Shallow breathing
- Lethargy
- Anorexia
- Weight loss
- Weakness
- Kidney dysfunction
- Blue or purple coloration of the skin
- Feather picking
- Regurgitation
- Paleness in the mucous membrane
- Excessive consumption of water followed by urination to flush the toxins out.
- Inability to balance.

The most common sources of infection are the cages, toys and wires around the cage that are galvanized, Washers or nuts made from zinc, pennies that were minted after the year 1983.

Lead poisoning

Lead poisoning is more fatal, as the lead that is absorbed will be retained in the soft tissues of the body. This can cause neural damage and can even lead to problems with the kidneys and the GI system.

The symptoms of lead poisoning are the same as zinc poisoning, but the sources of zinc poisoning are a lot more in comparison. The common sources are toothbrushes, lead paint, lead weight used for curtains, crystal, cardboard boxes, dyes used in newspaper, vinyl or plastic material, stainless glass windows, plumbing material, foils of some champagne bottles, etc.

To treat this condition, an injection called Calsenate is administered. This acts like an antidote that will remove the zinc or lead that has entered the body. If the bird has ingested any metal object, it can be removed surgically. The bird must be put on a recommended diet to ensure that the kidneys and the liver does not shut down, making it harder for the metals to be eliminated from the body.

Make sure that your bird is in a safe environment in order to prevent any metal poisoning. If you are unsure of how to do this on your own, you have several professionals who can come to your home and take care of the whole bird proofing process for you.

5. Nutritional Diseases in Blue and Gold Macaws

It is very important that you provide your bird with proper nutrition. This is one of the most important concerns for most pet owners, avian vets and breeders. Avian nutrition has improved greatly in the past. However, there are still several birds that are just poorly or inappropriately fed.

There are two common reasons for improper nutrition in birds. First, giving the bird a choice in foods. If you give him a variety of foods at the same time, he is likely to only eat the foods that he likes. Second, giving them a seed only diet can also lead to malnutrition in birds.

There are various illnesses in birds that are a result of improper nutrition. Hepatic diseases, renal insufficiency, musculoskeletal conditions, respiratory issues, etc. are all caused by compromised nutrition in birds. The most common nutritional diseases in birds include:

Obesity

This is very common in birds that are kept at home. Owners allow the birds to overindulge. They will feed them a seed rich diet, table foods and lots of treats. In addition to this, if your bird is not getting sufficient nutrition, he will become obese. If your Blue and Gold Macaw is 20% over the recommended weight and has a 4/5 keel score, he is obese. Blue and Gold Macaws are among the highest prone pet birds to obesity. There are a few clinical signs such as obvious fat around the belly region, inability to walk properly and strained breathing.

It is a good idea to convert these birds to a pellet diet. You also need to control the portions of the food that you give your bird. Make sure that he gets a lot of exercise with toys or even by placing multiple bowls for food.

If your bird is capable of flight, you can also get him a large flight cage and leave him there for a few minutes every day. Obese birds will develop conditions like fatty liver disease, cardiac diseases and artherosclerosis.

Vitamin A Deficiency

Vitamin A is one of the most important nutrients for immunity in birds. If your bird has hypovitaminosis A, there are chances that the gastrointestinal tract, the reproductive tract and the uropygial glands of the bird are affected. The common symptoms include conjunctivitis, sneezing, polyuria, polydipsia, poor feather quality, anorexia and feather plucking. The papilla near the cloaca are also blunt or absent. You will see white plaques in the eyes, mouth and the sinuses of the bird. In chronic conditions sinusitis, pododermatitis and conjunctivitis is observed.

Treatment of this condition includes treating the secondary infections first and then providing vitamin A supplementation. The bird should be given a good pellet diet as opposed to ½ pellet and ½ seed. You can use precursors of Vitamin A in the form of sprays over the food that you give your bird. If you are doubtful about the diet of your bird, consult your avian vet or have the food that you are currently giving the bird examined for the Vitamin A content.

Iodine deficiency

If your bird is on an all seed diet, this condition is very common. With fortified diets available these days, this condition is observed very rarely in the bird. If your bird does have iodine deficiency, you will observe strained breathing, wheezing and clicking because the thyroid puts a lot of pressure on the respiratory tract of the bird. You can add a drop of Lugol's iodine in the bird's water to help him recover from this deficiency. Changing the diet will help subside the symptoms and also rebalance the iodine levels in the bird.

Phosphate, Calcium and Vitamin D3 Conditions

Commonly birds that have a seed based diet will have an imbalance in the phosphorous, calcium and Vitamin D3 levels. You will also observe amino acid deficiency in these birds. The most commonly used treat, Sunflower seeds, is very low in calcium and high in fat. Although some people may tell you otherwise, Safflower seeds are more harmful for your bird as it contains large amounts of fat. It is best to give your bird a good, balanced meal and ensure that he gets a lot of exercise to stay in shape.

Metabolic Bone Disease

This condition is usually observed in younger birds. It is also caused due to an imbalance in the calcium and phosphorous ratio. If your bird is on a high seed diet, there is a good chance that the calcium levels will deplete drastically. Most indoor birds also fail to get enough sunlight, which leads to a deficiency in the vitamin D3 levels.

Birds with this condition display deformation of the bones, the vertebrae especially. You will also observe signs like seizures, depression, weakness, ataxia, tremors and repeated fractures. If your bird is in the breeding phase, the production of eggs reduces drastically and more embryonic deaths occur.

Iron Storage Problems

When excessive iron is accumulated in the liver, several diseases may occur. When the level of iron increases, the membranes and the proteins are damaged. This condition has been seen occasionally in Blue and Gold Macaws and is not as common as the other nutritional conditions. The most common clinical signs include dyspnea, ascites, depression, weight loss, distension in the abdomen, etc. Usually the heart, the liver and the spleen are most affected. This leads to several conditions like circulation failure.

Supplementing the food with fibers, tannins and phylates is best for the bird. You must also avoid Vitamin C supplementation, as it causes over absorption of iron.

You also need to be careful about the brands of foods that you choose for your bird. Sometimes birds may develop conditions related to the preservatives added in the foods that you choose. Keeping your bird physically and mentally stimulated will go a long way in ensuring that all the nutrients are properly assimilated. Try to give your bird as much natural sunlight as possible. These simple measures can prevent most of the diseases related to diet and lifestyle in birds.

6. Providing first aid

Unlike other pets like cats and dogs, even the simplest injury to a bird can be life threatening. The reason for this is that birds go into shock very easily. When this occurs, the cardiovascular system of the bird does not function properly, leading to a loss of blood flow to the vital organs. That is why the first step towards treating any injury or trauma to the bird is helping him calm down. If you see that your bird has had an accident, take him to a quiet room and leave him there with some water. Make sure that you do not panic or scream in front of the bird. This makes it worse for him. Let him calm down and then you can talk to him in a calm and comforting voice. Of course, if the injury is serious, you need to take the bird to the vet immediately. Here are some common accidents that your bird may encounter and the necessary measures you have to take:

- **Skin wounds:** If the bird has cuts or bruises on the skin, wash it gently with 3% hydrogen peroxide. You can use gauze, q-tips or cotton to clean the area. In case the skin wound is caused by a cat or dog bite, wash the area and rush the bird to a vet, as their saliva is dangerous for birds. In order to stop bleeding in the skin, you can use a styptic pencil or you can also use cornstarch.

- **Bleeding nail or beak:** Sometimes, the bird's beak or nail can get entangled in the wires used to hang toys. It could also get caught in the bars of the cage. Then, you need to apply pressure on the injured area directly using a paper towel or cotton gauze. If that is not good enough, you can use a styptic pencil or cornstarch to control bleeding.

- **Broken blood feathers:** Bleeding in the broken blood feathers is profuse and can even be fatal if you do not curb bleeding immediately. Use a styptic pencil to clot blood and hold the area down with gauze or clean tissue paper.

- **Burns:** If your bird suffers from burns due to a hot stove, hot water, steam or even hot utensils, you can relieve the pain by misting the feathers with cold water. If the leg or foot is burnt, just dip it in cold water. Make sure that the water is not too cold. It should be cold water from the tap, not the refrigerator. You can use an antibiotic cream, but make sure that it is not oil or grease based as the heat is retained by such creams. In the case of acid burns due to cleaning agents or detergents, flood the area with lots of cold water to relieve the pain.

- **Heatstroke:** The best thing to do would be to put the bird in an air-conditioned room. If you do not use air conditioning in your home, you can use cold water to mist the feathers and then turn on a fan. If you are turning a fan on, make sure that the bird is in a cage. Then, give the bird water to drink. In case of extreme heat strokes, it might become necessary to drop water into the bird's mouth directly.

- **Broken bones or wings:** It is best that you do not handle a bird with broken bones. This may happen by flying into a window, predator attacks, getting caught between a door, etc. In the case of a broken wing, you can hold the wing close to the body and secure it before transferring the bird to a travel cage. You need to remove any perch or toy from the cage if you are transporting a bird with broken bones. Line the floor with a soft towel with no loops to keep the bird secure throughout the journey.

In case of any emergency, you can contact:
- In USA, ASPCA- 1-888-4-ANI-HELP
- In UK, RSPCA- 0844-453-0117

These services will provide you with immediate care for your bird. When you are not sure how to deal with a situation, it is best that you either give them a call or give your vet a call. If you are unsure about handling an emergency, you can make the situation worse for your bird. The only thing you need to do then is make sure that you stay calm and keep other people away from the bird until you are able to get some help.

First Aid Kit for Birds
In order to provide timely care for your bird in case of an emergency, you need to have an emergency kit ready at all times. Here are a few things that you must include in your first aid kit:

- A blood coagulant: This helps prevent any profuse bleeding. A styptic pencil is the best option. If that is not available, you may use cornstarch or even flour.

- Tweezers: The bandages that you use for your bird will be very small in size. Having a pair of tweezers makes it easier for you to handle them.

- Cotton swabs: Any time you need to clean up a wound cotton swabs will come in very handy. If you do not have any, you can even use Q-tips.

- Gauze: You need gauze to clean and wrap cuts, bruises and even bites. Sometimes, it also helps secure broken wings or bones.

- Bandages: If you want to have bandages in your bird's first aid box, make sure that they are non-adhesive. Specialized bandages are available for birds in most pet stores.

- Syringe: You will need a syringe to wash small wounds or the eyes of the bird.

- Disinfectants: The best option is hydrogen peroxide as it removes any germs that might cause infections to your bird.

- Towel: An injured bird can get aggressive and irritated. So using a towel to handle him will make things a lot easier for you.

Keeping a first aid handy is important. Also make sure that you are checking the contents for cleanliness and hygiene. If you notice that the bandages are dirty or dusty, replace them.

7. Is insurance necessary?

The medical needs of your bird can get quite expensive. Each visit will cost you anything between $50-100 or £25-50. If the bird needs medical attention and treatment, you may have to shell out a lot of money.

Insurance for pet birds is not that common. There are a few options available. However, it is best that you keep a separate account that you save some money in each week just for the medical care of your bird.

The two most popular insurance plans for parrots are:

- Pet Assure: With this policy you can only have your bird checked by a vet in the network approved by them. If your vet is not part of this network, you need to find one that is or you will not be able to get the cover for vet costs.

- VPI: This insurance does allow you to see any preferred veterinarian. However, they do put a limit on the number of visits and the cover that they offer annually. So, you may not be able to get full coverage for any major procedure that your bird may have to undergo.

The most common things that are covered by popular pet insurance are:

- Veterinary charges: They will pay for certain diagnostic procedures like X-rays and even some consultation fees. Veterinarian costs will most include emergencies only. With birds like the macaw that have long lives, there may be a limit on the cover offered annually that may go up to $1500 or £3000.

- Escape or Loss/ Death: If you lose your bird to theft or death, they may cover some amount of the market value of an exotic bird. Theft and Escape cover requires you to fulfill some security conditions such as purchasing a five-lever lock for the cage door.

- Public Liability: This covers any damage cause by your bird to another person or property.

- Overseas covers: This is necessary for you to travel with your pet to some countries.

The cost of your insurance with all these covers will come up to about $150 or £280 a month. These covers are purchased separately and you can cut costs on things like overseas cover or public liability cover if you do not think that it is necessary. However, all these covers are highly recommended for all pet owners. You can compare the costs of various insurance plans online to find one that works for you. If you have multiple birds, some of them may also offer a 10% discount on the insurance cover.

8. What is a health certificate?

Getting a health certificate from your breeder or the pet store that you buy from can save you a lot of trouble. With a health certificate or a health guarantee, you can be certain that you are not bringing home a bird that is already sick.

A health guarantee is only valid if your bird has been tested by an avian vet within 72 hours of you taking the bird home. If your breeder insists that you see a specific vet, it is a cause for worry as they may have some mutual understanding. You will get a guarantee after the doctor confirms that the bird does not have any health issues.

A health guarantee will have a few terms and conditions that you need to read very carefully. Here are some of the common clauses that you will find in a health guarantee.

- The bird must be thoroughly examined by an avian vet with 72 hours of purchase.

- The guarantee does not cover any veterinary costs.

- If the bird is diagnosed with any health issue in the first check-up, the pet store or breeder will replace the bird or will pay you back the entire amount that you paid for the bird.

- Any injury caused to the bird under your care is not covered by a health guarantee.

- Any health issues caused to the bird under your care are not covered by a health guarantee. This includes any form of stress, irresponsible husbandry, ill treatment of the bird and accidents

- Behavioral issues and psychological issues are not covered by the health guarantee.

- Any purchases you make while buying the bird such as cage and food is not included in the refund. You will only get a refund that is limited to the price that you paid to buy the bird.

Normally, parrot health guarantees are valid for a period of 90 days. In this time, if the bird develops any problems despite proper health care, the money, or a portion of it is returned to you. The later you take the bird to the vet, the lesser refund you get. For instance, if you return the bird after 3 days, you will get 70% back on the initial price of the bird. It you return the bird after 5-6 days, you will get 50% and so on. This is done to ensure complete fairness to both the owner and the breeder or the pet store owner.

Remember that a health guarantee is very different from a health certificate. The latter is necessary to obtain a license to keep your bird at home. You may also require it if you decide to travel with your bird. A health certificate will be given to you by a vet. Some breeders and pet stores also offer a health certificate at an additional cost of up to $80. This is an important document, so make sure that you get one along with a health guarantee. Some pet stores may not give you a health guarantee, although it is preferable if they do. However, with a breeder, a health guarantee is a most.

Conclusion

When it comes to being a pet parent, it does not matter what breed or species you bring home. The objective is to make sure that your bird is well cared for and is healthy. Learn as much as you can about your bird by spending time with him and also reading up about the species as often as you can.

This book is the first step towards understanding the needs of your bird. Once you are comfortable, you can explore other ways to play and interact with your bird and even learn about what he really likes or dislikes. With Blue and Gold Macaws, the bond that you form is for a lifetime. This is what makes these birds so special.

Make sure that you work towards creating a beautiful journey with your bird. He will thank you with endless love and companionship. As you progress, you will realize that there is so much more to these birds than the way they look or the fact that they are really quick learners. With time, they really will become one of the most important members of your family.

Here is hoping that you and your beautiful Macaw enjoy a life filled with fun and adventure.

References

As mentioned before, the more you learn about your Blue and Gold Macaw, the better care you will be able to provide. Here are a few sources on the Internet that will provide you with updated information about these birds. Whenever you hit a dead end and are unable to figure out certain aspects of your bird's care, you can refer to them for reliable solutions and information.

Note: at the time of printing, all the websites below were working. As the internet changes rapidly, some sites might no longer be live when you read this book. That is, of course, out of our control.

www.blogs.thatpetplace.com
www.cincinnatizoo.org
www.vetmed.tamu.edu
www.woburnsafari.co.uk
www.hhpz.org
www.looptt.com
www.parrotfeather.com
www.lafeber.com
www.australiazoo.com.au
www.fantasticpetcare.co.uk
www.seaworld.org
www.pets.thenest.com
www.animalcorner.co.uk
www.parrotsecrets.com
www.edmonton.ca
www.northernparrots.com
www.ducksters.com
www.parrotsdailynews.com
www.iucnredlist.org
www.petstation.com
www.birdbreeders.com
www.cites.org
www.allpetbirds.com
www.ncbi.nlm.nih.gov
www.oregonzoo.org
www.greyhaven.bc.ca
www.brightszoo.com
www.petcha.com
www.macaw-facts.com
www.bluemacaws.org
www.what-when-how.com

www.upatsix.com
www.animals.nationalgeographic.com
www.birdchannel.com
www.premiumparrots.com
www.lafeber.com
www.bagheera.com
www.thegabrielfoundation.org
www.peteducation.com
www.animal-world.com
www.madmaxmacaw.wordpress.com
www.fourleggedfun.blogspot.com
www.rainforestcruises.com
www.windycityparrot.com
www.studentswithbirds.wordpress.com
www.parrotislandinc.com
www.parrotsinternational.org

Published by Zoodoo Publishing 2018

Made in the USA
Coppell, TX
21 October 2020